Insect Biology
49 Science Fair Projects

Insect Biology
49 Science Fair Projects

H. Steven Dashefsky

TAB BOOKS
Blue Ridge Summit, PA

FIRST EDITION
FIRST PRINTING

© 1992 by **TAB Books.**
TAB Books is a division of McGraw-Hill, Inc.

Library of Congress Cataloging-in-Publication Data

Dashefsky, H. Steve.
    Insect biology : 49 science fair projects / H. Steven Dashefsky.
        p.   cm.
    Includes bibliographical references (p. 159) and index.
     Summary: Provides background and instructions for various projects
    related to the behavior, ecology, life cycles, and physical
    characteristics of insects.
     ISBN 0-8306-4031-2 (h)   ISBN 0-8306-4032-0 (p)
     1. Insects—Study and teaching (Elementary)—Juvenile literature.
    2. Zoology projects—Juvenile literature. [1. Insects-
    -Experiments. 2. Experiments. 3. Science projects.] I. Title.
    QL468.5.D37   1992
    595.7'0078—dc20   92-2347
                                                                  CIP
                                                                  AC

For information about other McGraw-Hill materials, call 1-800-2-MCGRAW in the U.S. In other countries call your nearest McGraw-Hill office.

Acquisitions Editor: Kim Tabor
Book Editor: Yvonne Yoder
Director of Production: Katherine G. Brown
Book Design: Jaclyn J. Boone
Cover Design: Holberg Design, York, Pa.

Dedication

To all the wonderful people I met and the friends that I made during my years at the University of Massachusetts in Amherst.

Acknowledgments

The author wants to thank Ms. Paul J.S. Martin for her technical assistance with performing the projects in this book and with the manuscript. Thanks also to Dr. John Edman for welcoming me back to Fernald Hall and Dr. Richard Merritt for the insect photographs on the back cover.

Workshops at your school

The author offers hands-on workshops and seminars for teachers on the projects in this book and many other topics. He can be reached at Sci-Tec, 383 Main Street, Ridgefield, Connecticut 06877, or call (203) 438-8080.

Contents

PART 2
INSECT ECOLOGY

PART 3
INSECT LIVES

PART 4

INSECT FORM AND FUNCTION

PART 5

INSECTS AND HUMANS

An introduction to insect biology

Insects are fascinating little animals. They are strange, wonderful, and truly amazing to study. They can live almost anywhere: from the driest desert, to the cold of the arctic circle, and in your home. They can be found in the soil, in the water, and flying through the air.

There are more kinds of insects on our planet than all other animals combined. In fact, roughly three out of every four identified animals on our planet are insects, and many scientists believe we have only identified a fraction of the total. Even more amazing than the number of different insects is the number of any one kind of insect. One female fruitfly in May can produce billions of fruitflies by September. Insects have incredible powers of reproduction! Additionally, most food webs would collapse if insects were removed from them. Insects provide us either directly or indirectly with food and other necessities of life.

However, while there are beneficial insects, there are also harmful ones. Many insects continually threaten our food supplies, and others transmit disease. Although many insect studies concentrate on ways to reduce insect pests, remember that for every pest species, there are thousands that are harmless or beneficial.

By doing the experiments in this book, you will learn to appreciate the benefits of these amazing creatures.

GETTING STARTED

Before beginning any of the projects in this book, be sure to read through this section. It provides important information that pertains to many of the projects, including selecting a field guide, identifying insects, making an insect collection, the proper handling of insects, and how to rear insects.

An insect field guide

It's an excellent idea to get an insect field guide. There is a list of these guides at the back of this book. Many can be found in your local and school libraries or purchased in a bookstore or science supply store. Field guides give you more than just pictures to help you match the insect to a name. They explain the traits that distinguish an insect from others, explain the insect's life cycle and behavior, and usually describe how to collect, preserve, and rear a particular insect.

Identifying insects

Once you have selected a science fair project and have an insect field guide, try to become familiar with the proper names of insects. Every experiment involving live animals should have the correct scientific name of the organism and an explanation of how it fits in with other similar types of organisms. With insects, using proper names is especially important because there are so many kinds of insects and there is so much confusion about their names.

Insects belong to the class Insecta. Different types of insects are grouped into *orders*. Insects with similar characteristics are placed into the same order. For example, beetles belong to the order Coleoptera and butterflies and moths belong to the order Lepidoptera. True flies (such as houseflies, mosquitoes, and fruitflies) belong to the order Diptera.

The orders are broken down into smaller groups based on even more specific characteristics called *families*. For example, the swallowtail butterfly belongs to the Papilionidae family, while the gypsy moth belongs to the Liparidae family. Families are broken down into smaller groups called *genus*, which contain insects very similar to one another. Within each genus are individual types of insects identified by their *species* name.

All organisms are identified by their scientific name, which consists of the genus and species of the insect. For example, the common housefly is *Musca domestica*, and you and I are *Homo sapiens*.

Even though scientific names might sound confusing, they never change. Anyone in any country can tell exactly what insect you are referring to when the scientific name is used. Common insect names on the other hand, are often confusing. For example, dragonflies and damselflies are not "true" flies, since they belong to the order Odonata, not Diptera. All insects are not bugs, since there are "true bugs" which belong to the order Hemiptera. Furthermore, all insects are not beetles because "true beetles" belong to the order Coleoptera.

When you research an insect, the best way to be sure you are gathering information about the correct insect is to use its scientific name.

Your field guide is the best way to become familiar with proper insect identification and scientific names.

Making an insect collection

An insect collection is a great part of any science fair project involving insects. All of the experiments in this book would benefit from a small collection of the insects involved in the project. The collection could include the insects used in the project or examples from each stage of the life cycle of the insect.

Collecting gear

If you decide to include a collection in your project, you'll need some collecting gear. First, be sure the field guide you are using has information on making a collection. See the end of this book for a list and a brief description of field guides.

You'll need an insect collecting net, such as a butterfly net for aerial insects or a *sweep net,* which collects insects in vegetation. These nets can be purchased in science stores or from a biological supply house, but you might be able to borrow one from your school. Biological supply houses are listed at the back of the book.

After collecting insects, you'll need an insect killing jar, which can be made or purchased. A killing jar is a container, such as a mayonnaise jar, with a lid that can tightly close and a substance at the bottom, such as plaster of paris, that can absorb fluid. An *activating fluid* is soaked into the plaster of paris. This activating fluid is a material that produces fumes to kill the insects.

If you want to build your own jar, follow these instructions: Fill the bottom of a mayonnaise jar with about 1 inch of plaster of paris and add water according to the instructions. Once the plaster is completely dry, pour 1 or 2 tablespoons of nail-polish remover into the jar. The polish remover, which is the activating fluid, should be completely absorbed by the plaster of paris. Do not smell the fumes from the fluid! Biological supply houses sell activating fluid as well as killing jars. If you make the jar but purchase the activating fluid, follow the instructions that come with the fluid. The fluid must be replenished occasionally, since it evaporates each time the jar is opened. The more the jar is open, the sooner the fluid must be replenished.

Collecting the insects

Large numbers of small insects can be collected with a sweep net in a field with tall (knee-high) vegetation. To sweep, move the net back and forth rapidly through the grass in front of you while walking slowly through a field. The net should be hitting the top few inches of the grass. Walk and sweep in this manner for about five minutes (FIG. I-A). To stop, flip the net closed by twisting the net opening downwards. This folds the net over the net rim and

I-A Numerous insects can be collected using a sweep net.

traps the insects inside. All the insects will be in the bottom of the net. After collecting the insects, place them in the killing jar for about one hour.

Small flying insects can sometimes be difficult to catch, so consider making or purchasing a *collecting aspirator*. This is a glass cylinder with rubber stoppers at each end. A glass tube sticks out of one end and a plastic hose comes out of the other end. You place the glass tube near the insect to be collected and suck on the hose at the other end. This sucks the insect into the cylinder. A fine net at the end of the tube ensures that you don't accidentally suck the insect through the tube and into your mouth (FIG. I-B).

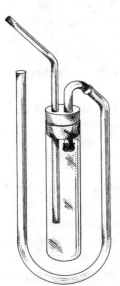

I-B A collecting aspirator is often used to collect small flying insects.

Large flying insects can be collected individually with a net. You can use tweezers or small forceps to pick up small insects that you find in wood, leaf litter, or a stream or pond. Insects can be found almost anywhere. Look in your field guide for more suggestions on how to collect insects.

Preserving and displaying your collection

How do you display the insects you've caught? Insects can be pinned and stored in a box, such as a cigar box, or they can be placed in *Riker mounts*, which are boxes filled with cotton and covered with glass. The cotton protects the insects, and the glass cover lets you view the insects within. Soft-bodied insects can be placed in vials filled with alcohol so they won't deteriorate. See your insect field guide for details on collecting, pinning, and mounting insects.

Handling and rearing live insects

Rearing insects and watching their development is a great way to study insect biology. The first requirement is a cage to hold the insects. Any tightly sealed container that has an opening for air will work. Glass jars work well because you can watch the insects through the glass. The opening must be screened so the insect can't escape. Nylon material, such as pantyhose, works well. Window screening is sturdier, but it won't hold in the very small insects such as no-see-ums or fruitflies.

Like all animals, insects need food and water. A good way to supply water is to soak a cotton ball in water and then place it on a nonabsorbant surface like a plastic bag. The insect can drink the water out of the cotton. A bowl of water would probably drown the insects.

The insect's food depends on the type of insect. Plant-eating insects should have a supply of their host plant. The host plant is the plant on which the insects regularly feed. Gather some leaves and twigs from the host plant when you collect the insects if you plan to rear them. Be sure to remember the plant's location, if you need to return for more. *Predatory* insects (insects that feed on other living animals) must be supplied with their live *prey* (the insects they feed upon).

While transferring small live insects into or out of a cage, it is hard to hold them with your hands or even with a pair of forceps without damaging them. The solution is a *transfer aspirator*, which is different from a collecting aspirator mentioned earlier. This is simply a plastic tube that you suck the insects into and then blow them out (FIG. I-C). A net at the end of the tube prevents the insects from being sucked into your mouth. Aspirators can be made or purchased.

WARNING: When handling live insects, remember that many can bite or sting. Be cautious! You should never handle an insect unless you are sure it

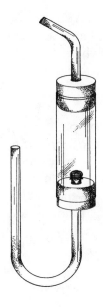

I-C A trasnsfer aspirator is used to transfer insects from one container to another.

is harmless. Do not handle any insects used in this book unless specifically instructed to do so. If you collect your own insects for an experiment instead of purchasing them, do not assume they are the same type of insect as described in the book. Use tweezers, gloves, or other handling protection as described in the book. Always work with an adult supervisor.

HOW TO USE THIS BOOK

Each of the 49 projects has an introductory paragraph, as well as a Materials, Procedures, Conclusion, and Going Further section. Each experiment gives you the step-by-step instructions, but leaves you to form a hypothesis and draw your own conclusions.

Introduction

Each experiment begins with an introductory paragraph that gives background information about the topic, explains the purpose of the experiment, and poses questions about the topic. These questions will help you develop a hypothesis for your experiment. Developing a hypothesis and the scientific method are discussed in more detail in the next section, "Science Fair Projects."

Materials

The Materials section lists everything needed to perform the experiment, but you can improvise when necessary. The following materials are not listed, but should be available for any of the projects: a pad and pencil for note taking, tape, scissors, and water.

Procedures

The Procedure section gives the step-by-step instructions on how to perform the experiment and suggests how to collect data. *Be sure to read through this entire section before undertaking any project.*

Conclusion

The Conclusion section doesn't draw any conclusions for you. Instead, it asks questions to help you interpret the data and come to your own conclusions.

Going further

This section is a vital part of every project. It lists many ways for you to continue researching the topic beyond the original experiment. Suggestions are given on what to read and what additional experimentation can be performed. Performing some of these suggestions can ensure that the topic has been thoroughly covered and show you how to broaden the scope of the project. The best way to ensure an interesting and fully developed project is to include one or more of the suggestions from this section of each project.

This book is designed for sixth- to ninth-grade students, but can be used by older students, as well. High school age students should include as many of the suggestions as possible to broaden the scope and depth of the experiment. Combining related projects is an excellent way to adapt these projects for older students. The final section of many projects suggests combinations with other projects.

Science fair projects

When selecting a science fair project, the first thing to do is find out what interests you about insects, if you don't already know. Begin exploring the world of insects by simply watching. Start by looking for insects around you: in your home, in your backyard, in the overgrown field down the street, or in the cracks in the pavement.

To tell insects apart from other small animals, just count the number of legs. Adult insects have six legs. Watch the insect's behavior. See how it finds food and how it acts with insects of the same kind or other types of insects. Look at the insect's body structure or investigate its habitat. If you find yourself saying, "I'd like to know more about . . ." you're well on your way to selecting a science fair project about insects.

The next step is to look through the contents in this book for more specific topics to research. This book contains 49 science fair projects about insect behavior, insect ecology, insect lives, insect form and function, and insects' significance to man. Read through the introduction to each project for additional information. Select a project that not only interests you, but excites you. Also keep in mind that some projects must be done at a certain time of year. Some experiments can be done in a day or two, while others can take a few weeks, and some even longer.

THE SCIENTIFIC METHOD

Science fairs give you the opportunity to not only learn about a topic, but to participate in the discovery process. While you probably won't discover something previously unknown to mankind (although you never can tell), you will perform the same process by which discoveries are made. The scientific method is the basis for all experimentation. It simply, yet clearly, defines scientific research. The scientific method can be divided into five steps: purpose, hypothesis, experimentation, research, and conclusion.

Purpose

What question do you want to answer, or problem would you like to solve? For example, how do ants warn their neighbors of danger? Can insects be used to control other insects, instead of using chemicals and, if so, how? The introductory paragraph of each project gives a number of questions and problems to think about.

Hypothesis

The hypothesis is an educated guess, based on preliminary research, that answers the question posed in the purpose. You might hypothesize that sound, sight, or chemicals are used by ants to warn their neighbors of danger. You can form a hypothesis about any of the questions given in the introductory paragraph of each project.

Experimentation

The experiment determines whether the hypothesis was correct or not. If the hypothesis wasn't correct, a well-designed experiment would help determine why it wasn't correct.

There are two major parts to the experiment. The first is designing and setting up the experiment. How must the experiment be set up and what procedures must be followed to test the hypothesis? What materials will be needed? What live organisms, if any, are needed? What step-by-step procedures must be followed during the experiment? What observations and data must be made and collected while the experiment is underway? Once these questions have been answered, the actual experiment can be performed.

The second part is performing the experiment, making observations, and collecting data. The results must be documented (written down) for study and analysis. The more details, the better.

The Materials section of each project lists all the materials needed for each experiment and the Procedures section explains how each experiment is to be performed. Suggestions are given on what observations should be made and what data should be collected.

Research

Begin this part of the project before starting anything else, and continue after the experiment results are collected. Read as much as you can about the topic you are studying. Use all sources available to you. Try to be the expert on the subject. Once the experiment is completed, analyze the results and see how the information you have learned compares with what is already known about the subject.

In addition to researching the primary topic, see the final section of each project for ideas on related topics to research.

Conclusion

Once you have collected and analyzed the data, and have researched the subject, you can draw your conclusions. Creating tables, charts, or graphs will help you analyze the data and draw conclusions from it.

The conclusions should be based on your original hypothesis. Was it correct or incorrect? Even if it was incorrect, what did you learn from the experiment? What new hypothesis can you create and test? You always learn something while performing an experiment, even if it's how *not* to perform the experiment the next time.

The Procedures section of each project suggests what observations to make and data to collect. The Conclusion section often contains empty tables to fill with your data, and suggests ways of analyzing the data. This book provides guidance, but you draw your own conclusions.

SCIENCE FAIR GUIDELINES

Most science fairs have formal guidelines or rules. For example, there may be a limit to the amount of money spent on a project or the use of live animals. Be sure to review these guidelines and check that the experiment poses no problems. Most restrictions about the use of animals do not pertain to insects, but confirm this with fair officials before proceeding.

A word about safety and supervision

All the projects in this book require adult supervision. Even though insects are all around us and are a part of our daily lives, care must be taken when observing and especially when handling insects. Don't assume an insect is harmless. Follow all instructions in the procedures, especially as they pertain to the handling of insects. The entire project should be read and reviewed by the child and the supervising adult before beginning. The adult should determine which portions of the experiment the child can perform without supervision and which portions will require supervision.

Part I

Insect Behavior

Behavior is simply defined as what an animal does. There are many types of behavior. Feeding behavior, grooming behavior, social behavior, and mating behavior are a few examples. Most insect behavior is *innate*, meaning insects are born to behave in a certain way, but some insect behavior is *learned*. For example, honeybees learn the way to get back to their hives. Both innate and learned behavior helps the insect survive, by choosing the correct food, or locating the correct kind of shelter, or even finding the right mate.

Behavior also includes how insects act with each other. Some insects can communicate with each other using chemicals, songs, or body language.

To study behavior you must chart the movements of an individual insect before, during, and after some event. The event could be the change of light to dark, a change in temperature, of habitat, of food, of neighbors, or a physical or chemical disturbance, called a *stimulus*.

When you study behavior and report the results, it is always important to be completely objective. Don't make assumptions about the reason for the behavior, just report the facts. Try not to draw conclusions from them. It's easy to say "the insect was unhappy" or "the insect loves the light," but these are assumptions.

The projects in this section cover a range of types of behavior, including how insects communicate, how insects react to a stimulus, how insects form social organizations, and how they use protective coloration. There are also projects on insect predators, parasites, and parasitoids.

1
Warning bells!
How aphids use pheromones as a warning

Aphids, also known as plant lice, live together on certain types of plant stems and feed by sucking up plant sap (FIG. 1-1). They insert their mouth parts into the plant and remain on the plant indefinitely. If left undisturbed, they'll likely spend their entire life at the same spot where they were born. But an undisturbed life isn't guaranteed for most aphids. They are one of the favorite foods for many insect predators and parasitoids.

Predators that love to eat aphids include ladybird beetles (or "ladybugs"), who march through the colony munching away on the aphids. Luckily, for the aphids, they can sense danger. When an aphid is caught by a predator, it gives off an alarm *pheromone*. A pheromone is a chemical that other members of the colony can detect. The other aphids are alerted to the danger by the pheromone. Aphids can't fight, so their only available reaction is to flee. They detach their mouth parts from the plant and drop to the ground.

How quickly do pheromones work? How far away from the injured aphid can the pheromones be sensed? Do all the aphids in the colony react the same way? State your hypothesis and proceed with the project.

MATERIALS
- An aphid colony covering at least 3 inches of a plant stem (You can find one in a local field or garden, or create your own by placing a bean plant outdoors in a very sunny spot during the summer months in most parts of the country. It will be naturally infested with aphids within a few weeks.)
- Fine forceps
- Good-quality ruler

PROCEDURES
This experiment can be done from spring to fall, when aphids are often found. Locate or create an aphid colony as described in the Materials section.

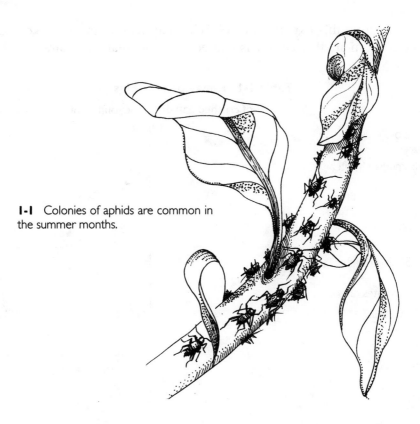

1-1 Colonies of aphids are common in the summer months.

Observe the aphid colony for a few minutes and watch their movements (if any). Record your observations. Do not touch or disturb the colony in any way while making your observations.

At the center of the aphid colony (midway on the stem), crush a single aphid with the forceps. This mimics the effect of a predator. Be careful not to disturb any other aphids as you do this. Quickly and carefully, observe the behavior of the aphids and write down your observations.

CONCLUSIONS

What was the reaction of the other aphids? How quickly did you see a reaction? Which aphids reacted? How far from the damaged aphid did this reaction occur? How long did the pheromone appear to have an effect? Fill in a table similar to TABLE 1-1. What are your conclusions?

GOING FURTHER

- Read more about pheromones.
- Consider doing the project *All hands on deck*, which is also about insect pheromones.

- To continue this experiment, see what happens if an aphid you've collected from another colony is injured. Does it create the same reaction?

Table 1-1 Behavior of aphids

	Within 1" of crushed aphids	Beyond 1" of crushed aphids
Before crushed		
Immediately after		
15 minutes after		
30 minutes after		
45 minutes after		
60 minutes after		

2
Singing sensations
Sound production and cricket behavior

Insects use sound in many ways. Sounds might be made in fear of a predator, to attract a mate, or to declare territorial rights. When and why do crickets make sounds? Do *all* crickets produce sound, or just one sex? Do crickets
only make sounds at a certain stage of their development? State your hypothesis and proceed with the project.

MATERIALS

- About 30 crickets of different sexes and at varying stages of their development. (The easiest way to get the entire collection of crickets is to go to
  a pet or bait store. These establishments often rear crickets as food for
  their other pets or for bait. You can also purchase them from a biological
  supply house.)
- 10 pint-sized, wide-mouthed jars
- 10 pieces of nylon material, such as pantyhose, to cover the jars
- 10 rubber bands to hold nylon on the jars
- 10 small plastic bags
- 10 cotton balls
- Spoon
- Oats
- Sand
- Watch with second hand

PROCEDURES

This experiment can be done at any time of the year. Each jar must be prepared to hold and maintain a cricket for a few weeks.

Put ½ inch of sand in the bottom of the jar. Put a plastic bag on the sand.
You can cut the plastic to create two-inch-square pieces. Take a cotton ball,
wet it very well, and place it on the plastic bag. The plastic keeps the sand
dry. This will be the cricket's water supply. You'll need to rewet the cotton

every two to three days. Put a teaspoon of oats, which is the cricket food supply, on the sand. Finally, label each of the 10 jars, "#1" through "#10." The jars are now ready for the crickets.

Before placing the crickets in the jars, you must be able to distinguish males from females and mature crickets from immature crickets. Both are easy to do. The female cricket has a long *ovipositor* (egg-laying device) coming out from the rear of its body (FIG. 2-1).

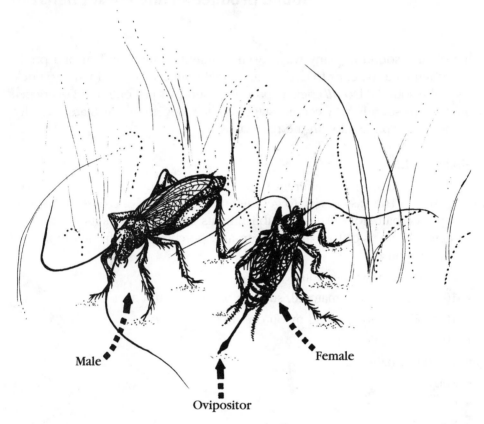

Male

Ovipositor

Female

2-1 A female cricket has a long ovipositor, while the male does not.

Mature crickets have fully developed wings, whereas immature crickets have *wingpads* that look exactly like what the name implies. The wings are short and not fully developed; they look more like pads than wings (FIG. 2-2).

Put the following cricket combinations into the following jars: (You can pick crickets up with your hand or use a forceps, but be careful not to squish them. You might want to put the crickets in their original container into the refrigerator for about 10 minutes to slow them down first.)

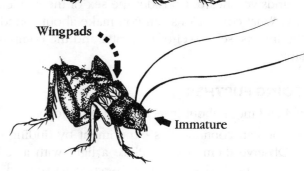

2-2 An immature cricket has wingpads, while the adults have fully developed wings.

Jar #1	One immature male (no wings, no ovipositor)
Jar #2	One immature female (no wings, ovipositor)
Jar #3	One mature male (wings and no ovipositor)
Jar #4	One mature female (wings and ovipositor)
Jar #5	Two immature males
Jar #6	Two immature females
Jar #7	Two mature males
Jar #8	Two mature females
Jar #9	Two mature males and one mature female
Jar #10	Two mature males and two mature females

After you place the correct crickets into each jar, close the jars with the nylon material and rubber bands. Put the jars in a room with natural light as the only light source. Do not use any artificial light in the room.

Every day, listen for singing. Listen at different times of the day and night. When you hear any sound, record which jar or jars it is coming from. Record the type of singing, the number of chirps per minute, and how long the singing lasts. Do not pick up the jars to do this. Continue your observations for about three weeks. Take diligent notes every time you make observations. This might mean noting that no sounds occurred in some jars.

Be sure to redampen the cotton balls every two to three days and add a teaspoon of fresh oats once a week. It might be easier to put some jars in different rooms, but be sure they all get the same amount of natural light.

CONCLUSIONS

After three weeks, compile all your observations and analyze the data. Consider the following questions: What did you hear from each jar regarding the type of sound, length of sound, and chirps per minute? Did you hear more than one kind of singing? Did the sounds from any one jar change over time?

After determining what sounds were produced from each jar, try to determine why the residents of each jar produced (or did not produce) the sounds you heard. Consider the sex of the residents and their level of maturity. What conclusions can you make about sound production as it relates to the insects' sex, level of maturity, and the combination of individuals in the jars?

GOING FURTHER

- Read more about insect sound production.
- You can continue this experiment by finding out how the crickets sing. Observe them closely. Place a light with a red bulb near some of your most vocal crickets. (Most insects can't see red, so the room appears dark to them and they cannot see you watching them.) Look closely at a chirping cricket and see if you can tell how sound is produced.

3

Voracious bugs
Biocontrol and predators

Many insects eat other insects. These insect predators are an important part of many ecosystems. Some of these insects are used by farmers to protect their crops against harmful insects. When an insect predator is used to control other harmful insects, they are called *biocontrol agents*. Using these biocontrol agents can reduce the farmers' use of chemical pesticides, yet still keep pest populations low. It can also save the farmer the cost of the expensive pesticides and is good for the consumers, since they don't have to worry about eating the chemicals in or on their foods. As environmental awareness increases, biocontrol is becoming more popular.

Before a biocontrol agent can be used, it must be thoroughly researched. What kinds of harmful insects can the agent eat? How many offspring can be produced? How fast do they reproduce?

Study the biology of the praying mantis (FIG. 3-1), which is a predator, to determine if it could be used as a biocontrol agent. How many praying mantises come out of a single egg case? How many insects can one newly hatched mantis eat in a week? State your hypotheses.

MATERIALS

- Praying mantis egg case (You can order these from biological supply houses or buy them at an organic gardening store. With some luck you can collect one outdoors.)
- Fruitflies (These, too, can be ordered from a biological supply house, or you can collect your own by leaving a fruit to rot outdoors. You can catch them with an aspirator when they land on the fruit.)
- One large, wide-mouthed jar (approx. 32 ounces)
- Three small, wide-mouthed jars (approx. 16 ounces)
- Nylon material to fit over the mouths of the jars
- Rubber band to fit around the mouths of the jars
- Cotton balls
- Transfer aspirator

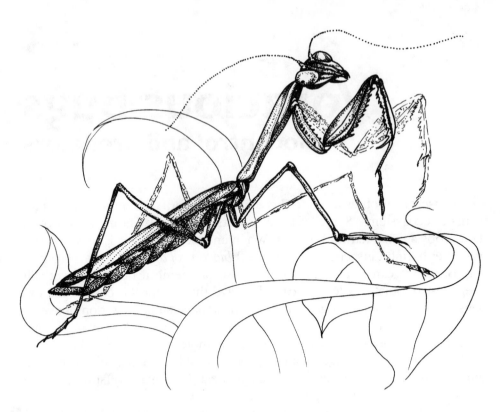

3-1 The praying mantis is a predator.

PROCEDURES

You can do this experiment anytime of year if you are ordering the insects, or from late summer to spring if you are collecting your own. Put the praying mantis egg case (along with the stem it came on) in the large jar and keep the jar at room temperature. Cover the jar with the nylon material and hold the nylon on tightly with a rubber band. Cut a small cross in the nylon material, and then stick a wet cotton ball halfway into the cage (FIG. 3-2). This will be the insect's water supply. You can add water by dripping it onto the outside of the cotton ball when it becomes dry.

Every day, check the cage to see if the young have hatched. Once they hatch, count how many there are. They will all emerge within a few hours of each other. You can open the top to count them since they cannot fly away. You might want to put the cage in the refrigerator for about five minutes to slow them down before opening the cage. How many mantises came out of a single egg case?

Now that you know how many can be produced from one female, how many insects can a mantis eat? Mantises will eat one another, so you should

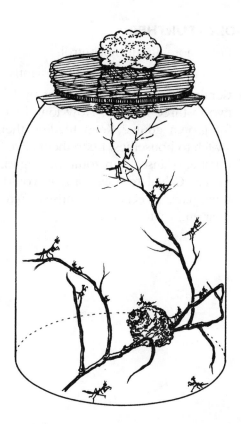

3-2 This is the setup that houses your praying mantis egg mass and the young that will emerge.

separate one individual from the others for this part of the experiment. Set up the smaller jar similar to the larger jar, with the cotton ball in the top. Place a few twigs in the jar so there is a place for the insects to land. You might want to have one or two additional jars like this.

Now, place 10 fruitflies in the cage with the single praying mantis. To do this, suck 10 from their container into the aspirator. Hold your finger over the end of the aspirator so they don't escape. Remove the cotton ball from the nylon cover and place the aspirator into the hole to release them into the jar. Replace the cotton ball.

Every day, count the number of fruitflies in the cage. Make note of how many are left each day. Replace those that were eaten each day so you maintain 10 fruitflies in the jar. Do this for at least two weeks to determine how many fruitflies a young praying mantis eats per week.

CONCLUSIONS

Now that you know how many young emerge from a single egg mass, and how much each young can eat, do you think they would make a good biocontrol agent? What are your conclusions?

GOING FURTHER

- Read more about biocontrol.

- Read more about the praying mantis's life cycle and its eating habits.

- Continue with this experiment by keeping some of the insects alive for two to three months. How long before the insects have developed into full-grown adults? Keep feeding them fruitflies. When they get bigger, switch to houseflies. Keep them alive for as long as possible. Compare the number of insects an adult praying mantis eats to that of a newly hatched mantis. Calculate how many it would eat over its lifetime. Then calculate how many insects the mantises from a single egg case would eat during their entire life spans.

4

Mother at work
Biocontrol and parasitoids

Parasitoids are insects that lay their eggs in other insects (the parasitized insect is called the *host*). The immature insect emerges from its egg inside the host and gets its nourishment from the host. The host dies and the parasitoid eventually emerges from it.

There are many kinds of parasitoid wasps. These tiny creatures are harmless to humans. Some species lay their eggs in the pupal stage of their host, others in the larval stage, and still others in the eggs of their host (FIG. 4-1).

There is often a direct relationship between the size of a female insect and the number of eggs she can lay. Since these wasps are so small, they have a limited number of eggs they can produce and must be very selective about where they lay their eggs. If they pick the wrong kind of host, their eggs won't survive. If they pick a sick host or a host that already has eggs in it, their eggs might not survive. To avoid wasting eggs, a female parasitoid must be able to sense the condition of a host, to tell how good it is for her offspring.

How does a mother parasitoid wasp sense a host? How does the mother determine where she should or should not lay her eggs? What is your hypothesis?

MATERIALS

- At least five newly emerged Trichogramma minutens wasps (These can be purchased from a biological supply house or from an organic gardening nursery.)
- 50 tobacco hornworm eggs, to use as host for the wasps (These must be ordered from a biological supply house.)
- One petri dish (or a dish about ½ inch deep × 4 inches diameter that can be closed)
- Straight pin
- Forceps
- Small paintbrush (like one used for painting model planes)
- Dissecting microscope, or a high-quality magnifying glass

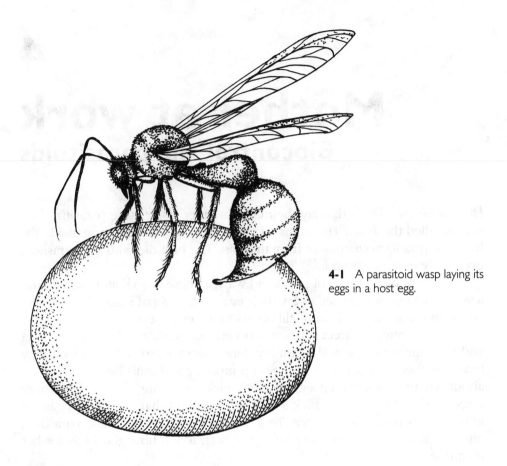

4-1 A parasitoid wasp laying its eggs in a host egg.

PROCEDURES

This experiment can be done at any time of the year. Take some tobacco hornworm eggs (about 20) and either crush them with the forceps or put a hole in them with a pin. You'll need to do this under magnification. Place these bad eggs and an equal number of good eggs in a petri dish. Keep the good and bad eggs separated in the dish, since you must identify them later.

Now, add about 10 Trichogramma minutens wasps. Use the paintbrush to pick up and move the wasps, but be very gentle since they are delicate. Or use an aspirator as described in the Introduction.

Watch their behavior under magnification. Watch how the wasps prepare to lay eggs. Watch how they walk over the egg. Record their movements on each type of egg, good and bad. Record how they touch each type of egg. What body parts do they use to inspect the eggs? Do they lay any of their eggs in the bad host eggs? How much time do they spend on the good eggs versus the bad? Watch the wasps for about one hour. Observe for 10 minutes out of every 20 minutes. Fill in a table similar to TABLE 4-1.

Table 4-1 Insect Behavior

Contact with eggs	Good eggs yes/no	Bad eggs yes/no
Touches eggs with:		
Antennae		
Mouth		
Legs		
Wings		
Tip of abdomen		
Egg laying observed:		
Percent of total time: spent on eggs		

CONCLUSIONS

What conclusions can you draw from your observations? Does the mother know what she is doing or does she leave the young's fate to luck? What parts of her body are used during her investigation of the host eggs? Can she tell a good egg from a bad egg? Was your hypothesis correct?

GOING FURTHER

- Read more about parasitoid and parasitic wasps.
- Read about how these and other types of parasitic and parasitoid wasps are used as biocontrol agents.
- Continue this experiment by placing 50 wasps with 15 good eggs and 15 bad eggs. Observe their behavior. What happens differently when the females are crowded together?

5
All hands on deck!
How ants use pheromones

Insects that live in colonies can communicate with each other in many ways. Honeybees dance to tell other bees the location of food and ants lay down chemical trails to lead other ants to food.

Ants and other insects use chemical substances called *pheromones* to communicate between members of their species. These pheromones communicate information about the health and welfare of the colony, indicating who is sick or hungry and if danger is present.

What is the reaction of an ant colony to the pheromones released when an individual of the colony is killed? How does the reaction differ when a different species of ant is killed? State your hypothesis and then proceed with the project.

WARNING: Ants can bite. Follow the instructions carefully. There is no need to come in direct contact with ants in this experiment. Some portions of the United States contain fire ants, which are very dangerous and must be avoided. If you live in an area where fire ants are present, don't perform this experiment unless you can identify and avoid them.

MATERIALS

- Ant colony (The easiest way to perform this experiment is to find an active colony of ants outdoors. If you prefer, you can buy a complete kit from a toy or science store, or you can build your own ant colony container by following the instructions at the end of this project. If you're not using a natural colony, live ants can be purchased as part of the kit or from a biological supply house, or you can collect your own ants by following the instructions at the end of this project.)

- A couple of ants of a different species or from a different colony (You can either collect your own by following the instructions at the end of this project, or purchase another type of ant.)

- Forceps

PROCEDURES

Buying or creating your own colony means you can perform this experiment at any time of year. If you plan to find a colony outdoors, the project must be done during warm weather.

Find an active colony of ants outdoors or create your own colony as mentioned in the Materials section.

Watch the normal behavior of the colony and take detailed notes. Take your time and observe as much detail as possible. What do the individual insects do? What body movements do they make and where do they go? How do the ants interact with one another? Do they touch each other or avoid each other? Write down all of your observations.

If you are using a colony that has been purchased, record the behavior of the colony when the lid or top of the colony container is opened and closed. This will assure that the observations you are about to make aren't due to the opening and closing of the top, instead of the test stimulus you will be creating.

Once you have finished observing this behavior, use your forceps to crush a single ant in the colony. To do this, lift the top off the colony, reach in, and crush an ant on the surface of the sand with the forceps (FIG. 5-1). If it's a natural colony, crush an ant on the soil near the opening to the nest. Watch the reaction of the colony as soon as this is done and document your observations. Did the behavior of the other ants change? Continue your observations until the colony's behavior appears to be normal.

Once this is completed, find an ant (or use the one you've purchased) of

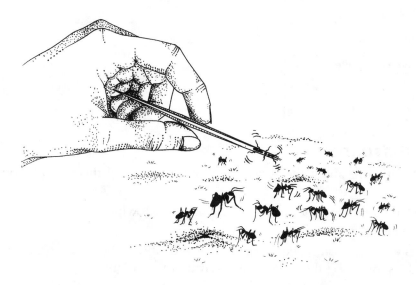

5-1 Ants produce a pheromone when injured.

a different species or at least from a different colony. Crush this ant with the forceps and add it to the colony. Write down your detailed observations.

CONCLUSIONS

What was the colony's reaction to the crushed ant from the same colony? What was the reaction when the foreign ant was crushed? Were the reactions different? If they were different, how were they different? Fill in a table (TABLE 5-1). Compare your notes and draw your conclusions. To fully understand exactly what happened, be sure to research more about pheromones.

Table 5-1 Colony behavior observations

Normal behavior	
Opening and closing top	
Native ant	
Before crushing ant	
Immediately after crushing ant	
10 minutes after crushing ant	
Strange ant	
Before crushing ant	
Immediately after crushing ant	
10 minutes after crushing ant	

GOING FURTHER

- Read more about the social behavior of ants and the role pheromones play.
- Consider doing the project, *Warning bells!,* which is also about insect communications.
- The colony you made or purchased probably didn't have a queen. How does this affect the long term survival of the colony?
- To continue with this experiment, add a live ant from another colony and observe the reaction of the ants. What is the reaction of the colony?

To build your own ant colony

If you plan to build your own ant colony, you'll need the following additional materials.

- A large clear jar with a wide mouth (A 32 ounce mayonnaise jar would work well.)
- A smaller wide-mouth jar that can fit inside the larger jar and leave a ½ inch to one-inch gap between the two jars. (A small mayonnaise jar would work.)
- Sand
- Sponge
- Honey
- Fine nylon netting, such as pantyhose, to cover the large jar opening
- Rubber bands to hold the netting over the large jar opening
- Small package of seeds (any kind)

Turn the smaller jar upside down and place it in the large jar. Pour the sand in the space between the two jars until it covers the inside jar (FIG. 5-2). Sprinkle the seeds on the sand's surface and then place 5 drops of honey on the surface of the sand for food. Cut a 1-inch-square piece of sponge, dampen it, and place it on the surface of the sand. This will be the ants' water supply. Cut a double or triple layer of the fine nylon netting so it can be used as a cover over the large jar mouth; use rubber bands to hold the netting in place. Be sure the cover is secure.

To collect your own ants for the colony

To collect your own ants you'll need the following additional items:

- Empty tuna can
- Honey
- Forceps to hold the can
- Gloves
- Large, heavy duty, zipper-lock plastic baggy to hold the can of ants
- A container with a lid that can hold the baggy, the can, and the ants

During the warm weather, you can collect your own ants by putting a teaspoon of honey in an empty tuna fish can and placing it outside. Once a large number of ants are in the can, pick it up using forceps with a glove on your hand and quickly put it in the plastic bag.

Place the plastic bag, can, and ants into a container with a lid such as a rubber storage container. Put the container (with everything in it) in the re-

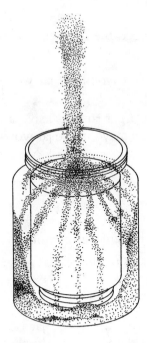

5-2 Create a homemade ant colony.

frigerator for 15 minutes to slow down the ants. Once the ants appear to be immobilized, shake them into the ant colony. Place the nylon cover over the jar and secure with rubber bands. Be sure it is sealed tightly. *Keep the colony in a safe place, but not in your home*, in case the container breaks or the ants otherwise escape.

To collect a foreign ant

Search for ants in an area at least 100 yards away from where you collected the original colony of ants. If you purchased the colony, it won't matter where you find the foreign ant. When you locate the ant, either slide a piece of paper underneath it and pick it up to place it in a small vial or simply trap it in the vial.

6

Breakfast of champions
Insect eating habits

Some insects eat almost anything, while others are very selective about what they eat. An important fact to understand about any insect's life is what it eats. What specific types of food does it eat and how wide a range of foods can or will it eat? We will perform this basic research on the common mealworm, which is the larval stage of a beetle. What types of food will a mealworm eat? Will it eat more than one type of food? What is your hypothesis?

MATERIALS

- 20 mealworms (can be purchased from a pet store)
- 10 containers (The bottom half of milk cartons would work well.)
- Nylon material to cover the containers
- Rubber bands
- 10 different foods: wheat bran, wheat germ, corn flakes, granola, white flour, whole grain flour, rice, bread, dead leaves, and a live plant (You can make a few of your own choices if you prefer.)
- Potatoes
- Knife
- Ruler

PROCEDURES

This experiment can be done at any time of the year. Use mealworm larvae all the same size (they should be less than ¾ inch long). Fill each container with 2 to 3 inches of food. Place two worms in each container. Put a slice of potato on top of the food as the worms' water supply. Cover the containers with the nylon material and fix it in place with rubber bands (FIG. 6-1).

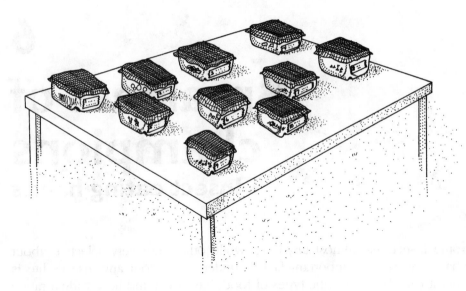

6-1 Test which food mealworms prefer.

You must replace the food and the potato every week. While replacing the food and water supply, you can collect the required data. To do this, gently shake out the contents of each container separately onto some newspapers. Put the same type of food back in each container, along with a new piece of potato. Find the larvae in the old food and measure their length. Record the length of each one, its overall appearance, and the date. Return the mealworms to the same container with the fresh food and potato.

Rear the insects to the pupal stage. (They will no longer have legs and their color will be much darker.) Depending upon the age of the mealworms when purchased, this may be a few weeks to a couple of months. Record the final length and overall condition of each insect. If an insect dies prior to the pupal stage, note its length and the date of its death. Fill in a table similar to TABLE 6-1.

CONCLUSIONS

Analyze your data. The length of the larvae and successful production of pupae are good indicators of whether mealworms could survive on the food they were fed. Did any mealworm thrive on one particular type of food? Did they do poorly on any particular type of food? If some of the foods weren't eaten, why were they not eaten? Do you think it was a matter of taste or a physical limitation that prevented them from eating the food? Did the food matter at all? What are your conclusions about the feeding habits of mealworms?

Table 6-1 Food number

Days	1	2	3	4	5	6	7	8	9	10
1										
2										
3										
4										
5										
6										
7										
8										
9										
10										
11										
12										
13										
14										
15										
16										
17										
18										
19										
20										
21										

GOING FURTHER

- Read more about insect food requirements.
- Read more about mealworms and their life cycle.
- To continue this experiment, adjust the amount of moisture in the foods they eat. Use the same food, but add varying amounts of potato slices to increase the water supply. Does this affect their survival?

7
Behave yourself
How insects react to a stimulus

Some of the most important scientific discoveries about insect behavior have come from simple experiments such as this one.

How does a mealworm react when a predator tries to eat it? Does it behave in a way to free itself? Does it always react the same way? Do different individuals of the same species react the same or differently? State your hypothesis and proceed with the project.

MATERIALS

- Five large mealworm larvae (purchased from a pet store)
- Two aluminum pie tins
- Forceps
- Stopwatch or watch with a second hand

PROCEDURES

This experiment can be done at any time of the year. Your observations are the most important part of this experiment. When observing the insect's behavior, watch its movements carefully. Notice whether it is moving its head or abdomen. Is it using its antennae? Is it crawling slowly or rapidly? Which direction is it moving (right, left, forward, backward), as well as the time it spends performing any of these movements. Write down the observed behavior in detail. This is a critical part of the experiment.

Begin by observing the reactions of a single mealworm when it's placed in an empty pie plate and left undisturbed. What does it do? Watch it for about 10 minutes and write down the movements it makes in a chart (TABLE 7-1).

Once you have completed observing the mealworm without any stimulus, perform the next part of the experiment. Disturb the mealworm in the way a bird predator would, by picking it up with your forceps (FIG. 7-1). (The forceps represent the beak of a bird.) Write down its reactions (behavior) to being picked up. How does it move? Continue writing down your observations in the chart.

Table 7-1 Behavior of individual

Situation	Number 1	Number 2	Number 3
Undisturbed			
Picked up (1st time) (immediate)			
Picked up (after 30 sec)			
Placed back down			
Picked up (2nd time) (immediate)			

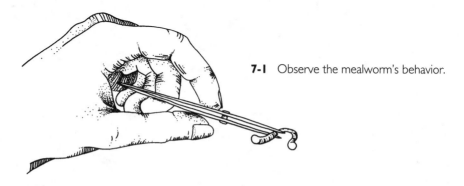

7-1 Observe the mealworm's behavior.

After one minute, drop the insect (as if it had freed itself from the bird's beak) into its container and continue to observe its behavior. If it falls from the forceps before the minute is up, that's fine. How does it move once it is free? Is its behavior different when dropped compared to its normal, undisturbed behavior you noticed at the beginning of the experiment?

Leave the insect undisturbed for at least ten minutes. Is there a change in behavior from when the worm was first released and ten minutes later? Repeat this entire procedure at least three times with the same mealworm. Does it always react the same way, every time?

After completing the procedure for the first mealworm, repeat the entire process with each of the remaining individuals. Be sure to keep track of those mealworms that were already tested by placing them into a separate container.

CONCLUSIONS

Study the results for each individual and analyze your observations. Next, compile all of the observations. Is the behavior the same for all five mealworms or did each react in a unique manner? Are mealworm reactions the same for all members of the species? What are your conclusions?

GOING FURTHER

- Read more about insect behavior. How do different types of insects escape danger?

- Consider doing the projects *All hands on deck* or *Warning bells!* also, since they, too, are about insect behavior when confronted with danger.

- Continue this experiment by trying the following experiment. Animals can get used to a disturbance; this is called *habituation*. Constantly pick up a mealworm and drop it. Don't let it rest between pickups. After you continue this for awhile, does the mealworm change its reaction behavior? Does it become habituated to the disturbance?

8
Lost on earth
Does protective coloration work?

Insects are tasty morsels for many animals. Birds, rodents, spiders, other insects, bats, bears, fish, and even humans eat insects. Insects use many methods to defend themselves against these predators. Fast flight, fast reaction time, protective casings and repellent chemicals are just some of the ways. Many insects use the simplest method of all. If they can't be seen, they won't be eaten.

Many insects have evolved colors that let them blend in with the color of their environment. A spectacular example of this is the walking stick. This insect looks and moves exactly like a stick or a small branch on a plant. Less dramatic, but more common, are insects that simply match the color of their habitat. Does matching the color of the habitat reduce the likelihood of being seen and eaten? What colors are most effective against what background? State your hypothesis. This experiment does not involve any live insects.

MATERIALS

- Dry, tri-colored macaroni which will represent insects of different colors (They should be spiral or elbow shapes, with one color being green. You can purchase colored macaroni at the grocery store, or you can make your own by cooking the pasta according to the directions on the box and adding food coloring while cooking. If you make your own, make some green, some brown, and a few bright colors such as red, blue, and orange. Air dry the colored macaroni and you're ready to go.)
- Paper lunch bag
- A lawn or meadow with short growth
- Yardstick
- String
- Watch with a second hand

PROCEDURES

This experiment can be done at any time of the year, as long as the lawn or meadow isn't under snow. Count out 20 pieces of macaroni of each color. Put them in the lunch bag and shake them well to mix them up. On a stretch of lawn, measure off a six foot square and mark its boundary with string. Have another person randomly spread the macaroni within this area, while you are not looking. With another person timing you, pick up as many pieces of macaroni as you can in one minute. At the end of the minute, count the number of each color of macaroni you picked up. Repeat this procedure 3 times and then reverse roles and have your assistant perform the experiment and you do the timing (FIG. 8-1).

8-1 Searching for macaroni "bugs."

CONCLUSIONS

Was one color collected more or less frequently than another? What was the relation between the most commonly collected macaroni and the color of the field or the meadow? Is your hypothesis correct?

GOING FURTHER

- Read more about the protective coloration of insects.

- Consider also doing *Color me green,* which also researches protective coloration in insects.

- Continue this experiment by breaking white bread into pieces and soaking them in different food coloring. Make the same number of each piece. Let them air dry. Mix all the colors together and then randomly place them outside in the same plot as in the original experiment. Leave the area and observe from a distance. Wait until some birds land and begin feeding on the bread. Let the birds feed until about half the bread is gone. Go out and count how many pieces of each color were eaten. If the bread represented insects of different colors, which would have been eaten? Was your hypothesis reconfirmed?

9
Color me green
How common is protective coloration

Insects are one of the favorite foods of many animals. Many insects protect themselves from predators by *protective coloration,* meaning they have colors that help them hide in their habitat. If they blend in with their surroundings, then predators that depend on eyesight to catch them may not be able to find them. Do the majority of insects blend in with their environment? What colors are most of the insects found in a field or in the soil? Is protective coloration common in the insect world? State your hypothesis and proceed with the project

MATERIALS
- Insect collecting net
- Simplified killing jar (Instead of creating a killing jar as described in the Introduction, you can use a 32 ounce glass jar with a screw-top lid and a cotton ball soaked in nail polish remover as the activating fluid.)
- Activating fluid (nail polish remover containing acetone)
- Cotton balls
- Large white piece of paper
- Tweezers or forceps
- Heavy gardening gloves

PROCEDURES
This experiment can be done from spring to fall. Find a grassy meadow or field that has not been mowed for a few weeks. The vegetation should be more than ankle high for best results.

While in the field, prepare the killing jar. Saturate a cotton ball with nail polish remover, so it's damp but not dripping. Put the ball in the jar and close the lid on the jar tightly. You now have an activated killing jar.

Sweep the field or meadow with the net to collect insects living in the vegetation. To sweep, move the net back and forth rapidly through the grass in front of you while walking slowly through the meadow. The net should be hitting the top few inches of the grass. Walk and sweep in this manner for about five minutes. To stop, flip the net closed by twisting the net opening downwards. This folds the net over the net rim and traps the insects inside. All the insects will be in the bottom of the net.

To immobilize the insects, grab the net with your hand above the bundle of insects at the bottom of the net. Insert the bottom portion of the net which contains the insects and the net itself into the killing jar. Hold the lid tightly over the mouth of the jar for a few minutes (FIG. 9-1). The net will be protruding from the jar, so you won't be able to close it completely. After a few minutes the insects will be motionless.

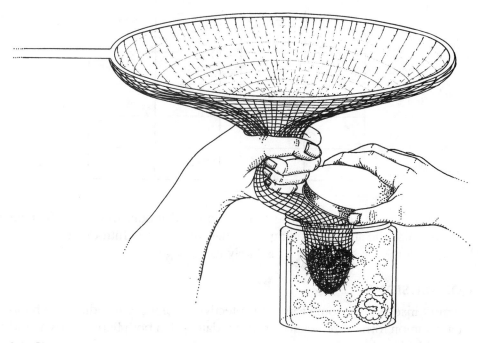

9-1 Place the portion of the net containing the captured insects directly into the jar while holding the top over the jar.

When the insects are no longer moving, dump them into the killing jar and leave them there for about one hour. Pour the collection on the white paper. Separate them by color. Count each color group. Is one color more common than others? Take detailed notes.

For the next part of the experiment, locate an area with rich, fertile soil, such as a garden, or in an area with a lot of leaf litter, such as in the woods. Using forceps, pick out any insects or other arthropods that you can find on or in the soil or leaf litter and place them in the killing jar. After about one hour, pour them onto white paper and separate them by color. Count each color group. Is one color more common than others? Take notes and fill in a table (TABLE 9-1).

Table 9-1   Color chart

Color	Sweep 1		Sweep 2	
	Number collected	Percent of total	Number collected	Percent of total
Brown				
Blue				
Yellow				
Green				
Red				
Orange				
Black				

If you plan to create an insect collection and mount the insects you've collected, use the standard killing jar as described in the Introduction of this book, because the simplified jar is likely to damage the insects.

CONCLUSIONS

Do most insects have some form of protective coloration? Is hiding in a habitat a common form of protection from predators? Do both habitats (lawn and soil or leaf litter) confirm your hypothesis?

GOING FURTHER

- Read more about insect protective coloration.
- Research why some insects such as bees, wasps and butterflies are brightly colored. Is this a form of protective coloration or some other adaptation for survival?
- Continue this experiment by finding insects that inhabit certain types of plants and flowers. Do the insects hide or want to be seen?

Follow the leader
Chemical communications of ants

There are insects (termites, honeybees, ants) that live together in large nests or hives. These are called social insects. They cooperate in food gathering, defense, rearing of the young, and all aspects of life. One of the most important requirements in this cooperation is communication. Imagine trying to build a home with ten other people if no one could understand what the others were doing. People can use spoken language or sign language to communicate with one another, but obviously, insects cannot speak. Instead, they use other forms of communication.

Many insects, including honeybees and ants, use chemicals to communicate with one another. When an ant finds a food source she leaves a chemical trail on the ground to lead her and the rest of the colony back to the food. This chemical trail contains information. Does the chemical trail an ant creates simply show a path between the food and the nest, or does it also indicate direction?

WARNING: Ants can bite. Follow the instructions carefully. There is no need to come in direct contact with ants in this experiment. Some portions of the United States contain fire ants, which are very dangerous and must be avoided. If you live in an area where fire ants are present, don't perform this experiment unless you can identify and avoid fire ants.

MATERIALS

- Four pieces of flat cardboard (about 8 inches × 10 inches)
- Honey
- Two or three active colonies of ants that you've located outdoors

PROCEDURES

This experiment must be done in the late spring to fall, when ant colonies can be found. Locate a colony, or just a trail of active ants. Put a large spoonful of honey a few feet away from where the ants are active, preferably on a hard surface such as a sidewalk. Surround the honey on all four sides with the flat cardboard pieces. Arrange them so any trail to the honey must pass over at least a portion of the cardboard (FIG. 11-1).

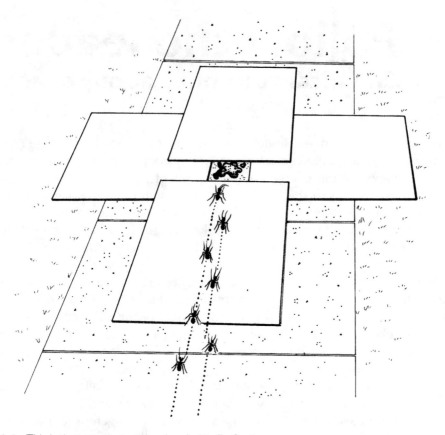

11-1 This is the setup to test the chemical trail of ants.

Soon, one or more of the ants will find the honey and create a trail to it. After awhile, the ants will form a trail leading to the honey that should pass over a piece of cardboard.

Record the behavior of the ants on the trail for at least ten minutes. Write down your observations. Once there are at least 30 ants coming and going over the cardboard, pick up the cardboard and turn it around so the path has been reversed 180 degrees. Do this quickly but gently so you don't disturb the ants. Wear protective gloves and don't let the ants crawl off the cardboard and on to you.

Once you have made the switch, observe the ants' behavior. Especially note the ants as they leave the cardboard and as new ones enter the trail onto the cardboard. What is their reaction? Compare it to the earlier behavior. Is there chaos or do they simply continue on their way? If there is chaos, how long does it take for the ants to reorient themselves? Take notes of your observations.

Repeat this experiment in three or four other areas, with different types of ants. Do you get the same results as the other colonies? Try to perform this experiment with different types of ants each time.

CONCLUSIONS

Can you conclude that the chemical trail not only indicates the path to take, but also the direction the ant is supposed to travel? Is this the case for all the species of ants you observed, or only a few?

GOING FURTHER

- Read more about how social insects communicate using chemicals.
- Continue this experiment by removing (and not replacing) the cardboard containing the trail and the insects. Observe the ants' behavior. How long does it take for them to recover?

Part 2

Insect Ecology

*E*cology is the study of how organisms interrelate with each other and with their environment. Insects affect, directly or indirectly, all living things on this planet. The reproduction of many plants is completely dependent upon insects. Insects are important in recycling nutrients and other chemicals through the ecosystem. In turn, insects are affected by other organisms and especially by man, often with devastating results.

12
To bee or not to bee
Insects' role in pollination

Plants that reproduce with seeds are the most diverse and abundant of all plants. Seed plants must be pollinated. Pollen can be transported from plant to plant by the wind, birds, and, especially for the flowering plants, by insects. Almost all fruit-bearing plants (including apples, pears, oranges, and strawberries) are normally pollinated by insects.

What happens if the flowering bud isn't visited by insects? Can some plants survive and reproduce without a visit from an insect? What is your hypothesis?

MATERIALS

- Two similar potted strawberry plants (These can be purchased at a nursery or even a supermarket. Cut off the runners of the strawberry plant to get good flower production.)
- Nylon material to cover one of the plants
- Sticks to prop up the nylon over one of the plants
- String or rubber bands that fit over the pots

PROCEDURES

Create a tent of the nylon material over one of the plants. The material must be light in color to permit sunlight to reach the plant, but it must prevent insects from entering. Tie the material securely around the plant with the string or rubber bands. You might want to use sticks to prop the nylon up and off of the plant, so insects cannot land on the nylon and still come in contact with the plant. Leave the other plant uncovered (FIG. 12-1).

Keep both plants side-by-side outside, but under cover, so rain won't damage the covered plant. Water both plants on a regular basis and care for them in the same manner. You'll have to open the netting to water the first plant. Be sure to rewrap it securely and quickly so no insects can enter.

Take notes during each observation. Do you see insects around the uncovered plant? What kinds do you see? After a few weeks, the plants should start to bear fruit. When this happens, count and compare the fruit on both

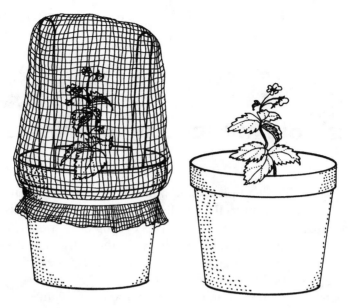

12-1   This is how to test the role insects play in pollination.

plants and record your observations. You might want to draw a sketch of each plant's fruit.

CONCLUSIONS

How do the plants differ? How many berries were found on each plant? What was the effect of blocking out insects during flowering? Are they necessary? What are your conclusions?

GOING FURTHER

- Read more about insect pollination. Which insects are the most common pollinators? Are there any bizarre types of pollination?
- To continue this experiment, see if all types of insects are good pollinators. Add a housefly or a ladybird beetle into another plant with a net cover. Can either pollinate the strawberry plant? Do all insects have the same effect on fruit production?

13
Life without insects
Insects' role in recycling nutrients

Insects help to recycle dead plants and animals. In any ecosystem, nutrients cycle from the living world to the nonliving world (when animals or plants die) and back again to the living world. This cycling of nutrients is necessary for the continuation of life. If this didn't happen, the nutrients of the dead organism could never be used again and sooner or later life on earth would run out of the basic building blocks of life.

Scavengers play a vital role in recycling nutrients. Scavengers are animals that eat dead creatures and return their nutrients to the ecosystem. Numerous insects are scavengers.

How long does it take for meat to decompose with and without the presence of insects? How important are insects in recycling nutrients? What is your hypothesis?

MATERIALS
- Two similar pieces of meat (same size, amount of fat, and bone)
- Two similar jars (quart-size canning jars, or 32 ounce mayonnaise jars will work nicely)
- Nylon material to fit in double layers over the mouth of one jar
- Two rubber bands to fit around the mouth of one jar
- Chicken wire or other strong mesh (It must be small enough to block out mice and other rodents but wide enough to let in insects. It must be stronger than window screening.)
- Wire
- Wire clippers
- Stakes
- Hammer

PROCEDURES
This project can be performed at any time of year, but will take much longer to complete in the winter than in warm summer months. Put one piece of

meat into each jar. Mark one jar "with insects." and mark the other "no insects." Put a double layer of nylon material over the top of the "no insects" jar. Attach the nylon with rubber bands. The other jar will have no cover.

You'll build a cage of wire mesh to keep the jars from being carried away by large animals. If you have a small animal cage made of wire and big enough to hold the two jars, you can use it instead of building this cage.

To build an envelope cage of chicken wire to protect the two jars, follow these instructions. Place the jars between two layers of the wire mesh. Tightly tie the edges of the envelope together with wire so the jars cannot be pulled out by animals.

Find a place outside to stake this envelope to the ground. It should be away from houses and out of direct sunlight. The area shouldn't be too moist. Hammer the stakes firmly through the edges of the envelope into the ground (FIG. 13-1). Record the date and time the experiment begins.

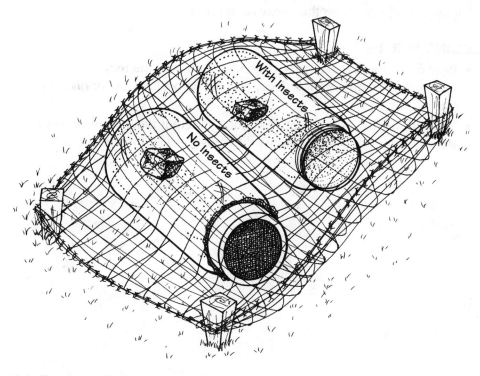

13-1 Test the role insects play in recycling nutrients.

Every one or two days, return to the jars and record your observations for each jar. Make observations on the condition of the meat and how much is left. What does the meat look like? Is it still solid? Are different portions (meat or bone), affected differently? Describe the presence of insects. When do you first see insects in the "with insects" jar? Hopefully, you won't see any in the other jar, or the experiment must be redone.

Once there is no further decomposition in the "with insects" jar, you can discontinue your observations. In summer, this experiment will last for two to three weeks. In the winter it could last for a few months.

At the end of the experiment, throw away the entire envelope. While wearing rubber gloves, pick up and enclose the envelope in a heavy-duty plastic bag. Tightly close the bag and put it outside with the garbage. Do not touch the decaying meat.

CONCLUSIONS

Study your observations. Compare the results for both jars. Did they decay differently and if so, how? Did the insects affect each portion of the meat (meat, bone, fat) in the same way? What conclusions can you draw about the importance of insects on the decay of the meat?

GOING FURTHER

- Read more about scavengers, decomposition, and the recycling of organic nutrients. How important is decay and decomposition to our planet's ecology?
- To continue this experiment, find out if different types of meat (beef versus chicken, for example) attract different types of insects.

14

Boat scum
The environment's impact on insects

Insects are often affected by the impact of humans on the environment. A few butterflies are on the verge of extinction because the plant species they need to survive are being lost to real estate development in rural areas. Certain species of tiger beetles and dragonflies are on the endangered species list because their habitats have been greatly reduced.

Although only a few insects are really in danger of disappearing from the face of the earth, many insects are affected by pollutants we produce on a daily basis. Aquatic insects are particularly sensitive to pollutants in streams and lakes. There are many sources of aquatic pollutants: industry, farms, highways, and cars are just a few. A typical example of this pollution is the trail of oil left on the water's surface by many motor boats. Can this thin film of oil affect insects living in the water? What is your hypothesis?

MATERIALS

- 15 mosquito larvae (These can be collected from a pond or from the water left in a container or old tire for a few days during the summer. If you can't find them, you can order them from a biological supply house.)
- Eyedropper with a tip that is not too narrow
- Measuring cup
- Flake fish food (from a pet store)
- Three similar containers (You can use one quart milk cartons, cut off at the bottom.)
- 3 tablespoons of vegetable oil (This will mimic the motor oil.)
- Teaspoon measures for ½ teaspoon and 1 full teaspoon
- Nylon material
- Rubber bands

PROCEDURES

Fill each container with 1 cup of water. Take a small pinch of the flake fish food, grind it up in your fingers, and drop it into the first container. Do the same for the next container. Don't use too much food.

Label one container "control," which will have no oil. Label the second container "#1." You want to cover about half the water with oil. Start by placing about ½ teaspoon of oil in the #1 container. Add more oil until the surface is half-covered FIG. 14-1).

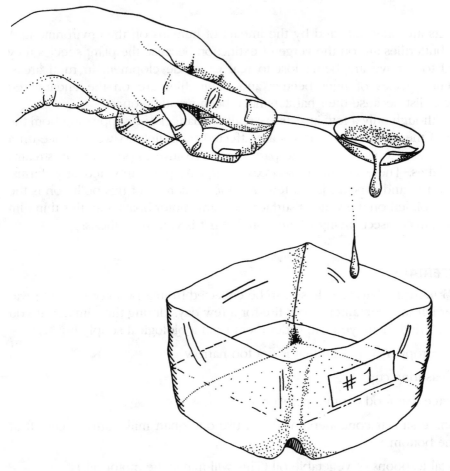

14-1 Pour vegetable oil into the container marked "#1" to cover half of the water surface.

Label the next container "#2." You want to cover the entire surface with oil in this container. Start with 1 teaspoon of oil, and add more if necessary. Use the eyedropper to place five mosquito larvae in each of these containers. Cover the containers with nylon material, and secure them with rubber bands. Record the start date and time and make careful observations about the mosquito larvae behavior.

Observe the containers every day. Record their activity and look for the emerging adult mosquitoes. They will be flying around in the container, under the netting. You can release them once they have been counted. Continue until adults are no longer found or the larvae have died (FIG. 14-2).

14-2 Mosquito pupae are odd-looking creatures.

CONCLUSIONS

What differences did you see in the mosquito larvae behavior in the jars? How many adults emerged out of each jar? Can the mosquitoes successfully pupate and emerge into adults if there is some oil on the water's surface? How about if the water is covered? Did the oil affect the mosquitoes' development? What are your conclusions?

GOING FURTHER

- Read more about the environmental impact of human beings on insects.
- To continue this experiment, repeat the procedure but use different aquatic insects. Collect or purchase water striders or water beetles and use them instead of mosquitoes. Use one jar without any oil, as a control, and the other covered with oil. Since these are adult insects, they won't develop, but see how they behave and how long they survive in both containers.

15
It's heating up
The effect of temperature on insect development

Insects are cold-blooded animals, meaning they cannot control their body temperature, so they are sensitive to temperature changes in their environment. Warm-blooded animals can control their own body temperature regardless of the temperature outside.

One of the pollutants man produces is thermal (heat) energy. Changing the normal temperature of an ecosystem can harm plants and animals, especially insects. Many insect life cycles are controlled by heat. Changing the natural amount of heat in an ecosystem can disrupt the timing of their life cycle with devastating effects. Different stages of an insect's life cycle can emerge too early or too late. If this happens they may not be able to find a mate, find their food, or eat enough food to survive through a season.

Is the development of the milkweed bug, (or crickets or mealworms) affected by increased temperature? If so, how are they affected? What is your hypothesis?

MATERIALS

- 50 milkweed bug eggs (available from a biological supply house)
- Unsalted, cracked sunflower seeds
- Two 1-quart-sized plastic ice cream containers with tops
- Knife with a pointed tip
- Petroleum jelly
- Four cotton balls
- Plastic sandwich bag
- Two lights with incandescent bulbs
- Thermometer

PROCEDURES

Set up two rearing cages. Take the plastic ice cream containers with their tops attached and make 15 small holes in the tops, using the pointed knife. These will be breathing holes for the insects. Now take off the lids. Put about 1 teaspoon of sunflower seeds in each cage for food. Saturate four cotton balls with water. Place two cotton balls in each of two open sandwich bags. Set each bag containing the wet cotton balls at the bottom of each cage. This will be the water supply for the insects. The plastic bags keep the food and container from getting wet and prevent the cotton from drying out too fast, but let the insects drink from them.

Take the petroleum jelly and put a thin film (½ inch wide) on the inside upper rim of the cage. This will prevent any insects from crawling out when the cage is open. Finally, place 25 milkweed bug eggs in each cage. Use a fine brush and forceps to move the eggs. Don't squash them.

Put one cage in a cool area such as in the basement. The temperature should not get below 60 degrees Fahrenheit, however. Put the other cage on a table with two lamps above it, so the light bulbs heat the cage (FIG. 15-1). Do not get the bulbs too close to the plastic containers. Keep them at a safe distance so there is no chance of causing a fire. Measure the temperature around each cage every two to three days.

15-1 How does heat affect insect growth?

Rewet the cotton balls every two to three days to make sure they remain moist. You will also need to replace the sunflower seeds each week. Sunflower seeds that have been eaten will be shrunken and turn color.

Observe and record the growth of the milkweed bugs each day. Measure the length of a few individuals every few days in each cage throughout their development to the adult stage. Adults have fully developed wings. Record body lengths as well as the date and the temperature. You can stop this experiment when at least two individuals from each cage have reached the adult stage.

CONCLUSIONS

What is the effect of the temperature on the growth rate? Does warmer temperatures cause slower or faster growth or is there no effect? If there are differences how might this affect the lives of the insects? What are your conclusions?

GOING FURTHER

- Read more about environmental factors that affect insect growth and development.

- To continue this experiment, study the ideal temperature range of the milkweed bug. Every insect has a temperature range in which they can grow and reproduce. If they develop in an environment below or above this range they won't survive. Can you discover the ideal temperature range for the milkweed bug? You need to rear milkweed bugs from the egg to the adult stage at a number of different temperatures. Perform the same experiment but place some containers in much colder environments and others in much warmer environments. What happens?

16

Who's in there?
Insects in the soil

Soil is a habitat that supports a tremendous number of insects. You might find hundreds of individual insects in a cubic inch of soil! As you can imagine, soil insects tend to be small. Soil is composed of minerals (*inorganic material)* and decomposing plants and animals (*organic material*). Different soils have different proportions of inorganic versus organic materials. Are all types of soils good habitats for insects? Do different types of soils contain different numbers and kinds of insects? What is your hypothesis?

MATERIALS

- Three lunch-size paper bags
- Garden trowel
- Three large funnels (quart size)
- Window screening (or similar screening)
- Three lamps with incandescent bulbs
- Three jelly jars (any 12 oz. glass jars)
- Three cardboard boxes (2- to 4 inches higher than the height of the jelly jars)
- Knife with pointed tip
- Rubbing alcohol
- Dissecting microscope or magnifying glass

PROCEDURES

You will collect three different kinds of soils and use an apparatus called a Berlese funnel to collect the insects inhabiting each kind of soil.

Find an area that has sandy soil (not beach sand). Find a dark, rich, fertile soil (humus), and soil in the woods with a lot of dead, decomposing leaf litter. In each area, use the garden trowel to fill a bag. Be sure to fill each bag from the different areas to the same height. Don't pack the material, just fill the bag. Close the tops of each bag tightly as soon as the soil is collected, and label each bag with the soil type, location, and date and time of collection.

Construct three Berlese funnels, like the one shown (FIG. 16-1). These are designed to collect insects living in soil. When the soil is heated with the lights, the insects move deeper into the funnel to get away from the heat until they fall out through the bottom of the funnel into a jar containing a preservative (alcohol).

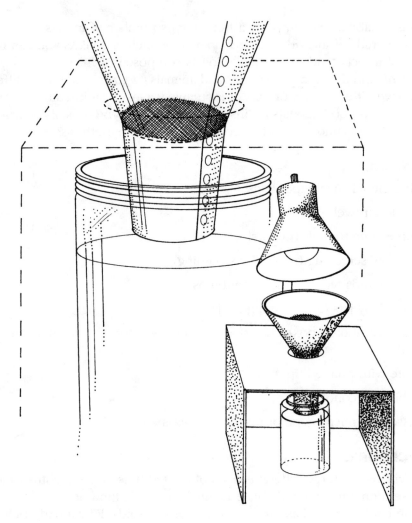

16-1 A Berlese funnel flushes out insects.

To construct a Berlese funnel, cut a hole in the top of the cardboard box so the funnel can rest in the hole. The size of the box should be carefully chosen, so that the tip of the funnel just enters the jelly jar opening beneath it. It should go about ½ inch to 1 inch into the jelly jar opening. The tip shouldn't go too far inside or it will be in the alcohol preservative.

Put a layer of window screen or similar mesh inside the wide opening of the funnel. Push it down slightly into the tip section so it remains in place. The screen keeps the soil from falling through the funnel, but lets the insects pass through. Fill the jelly jar halfway with rubbing alcohol. The alcohol kills and preserves the insects as they are collected. Place the jar under the tip of the funnel.

Set up a lamp so it's shining down on the top of the funnel. The bulb must be at least 6 inches away from the top of the soil. To prevent a fire hazard, keep the bulbs a safe distance from the cardboard. Label each Berlese with the type of soil about to be placed into it.

Once the funnel is set up, you can add the soil. Move the lamp out of the way and slowly dump the soil out of the bag, into the top of the funnel. Some soil will fall through, into the alcohol, but most of it will stay in the funnel. Put the lamps back in position. Do this for each of the three funnels.

Keep the funnels undisturbed for two or three days. Then, shut off the lamps and remove the jars. Use a dissecting microscope or a magnifying glass to count the number of insects in each collection. After you have counted the total numbers of insects, use your field guide and try to identify as many as possible.

CONCLUSIONS

What was the total number of insects collected from each type of soil? How many different kinds of insects did you collect in each? Are some soils better habitats for a variety of insects than others? Are some soils capable of supporting a greater total number than others? What are your conclusions?

GOING FURTHER

- Read more about soil insects. How are they beneficial to man and how are they harmful?

- Continue the experiment by using the Berlese funnel with additional soil types, or one soil type at different times of the year. You can also do the same experiment but vary the depth of your soil collection. How do the insect populations differ at the surface, at 2 inches, and at 4 inches below the surface?

17
Night nuisance
Night-flying insects

You come home on a hot summer night and quickly open and close the front door, trying to keep out the hordes of insects that have collected around the porch light. There are many kinds of night-flying insects: moths, mosquitoes, craneflies, dobsonflies, katydids, and the list goes on.

Night-flying insects are out from late spring until fall. Does the population of night-flying insects remain the same through the summer, or does it change over time? If it does change, what kinds of insects are present at different times? What is your hypothesis?

MATERIALS
- Insect collecting net
- Insect killing jar (See the Introduction for instructions on how to make or where to purchase this jar.)
- Cotton balls
- Zipper-lock plastic bags
- Porch light or other outdoor light

PROCEDURES

This experiment should be started between late spring and mid-summer. Every other night, collect insects that come to your porch light (FIG 17-1). They can be caught with a collecting net or caught directly in a jar. Collect at the same time each night (thirty minutes after full dark would be best). Place the insects in the killing jar and leave them there for a few hours.

Save each day's collection in a plastic bag that is labelled with the date, the time, and the weather conditions that night. Identify the insects collected on a regular basis using an insect field guide. Continue to collect for at least one month, and preferably two or more months.

Create an insect collection that represents the types and numbers of insects collected over time. For example, if you collected two types of moths in July and one was caught twice as often as the other, represent the more prevalent one with two moths and the other with one in the collection. Do

17-1 Create a collection of night-flying insects.

this for each week or month you were collecting. Disregard nights when it rained or was very windy. You are creating an insect collection that graphs the results (FIG.17-2).

CONCLUSIONS

What kinds of insects did you collect? How did the population change over time? How many of each did you collect? Did the numbers change over time? Did the overall numbers change or the numbers of any one kind of insect change? What are your conclusions?

GOING FURTHER

- Read more about night-flying insects.
- Consider doing the *Night flyers* experiment along with this project.
- To continue this experiment, add to your observations the temperature and humidity outside each time you collected. Analyze the results to see if these factors affected which insects were out at night.

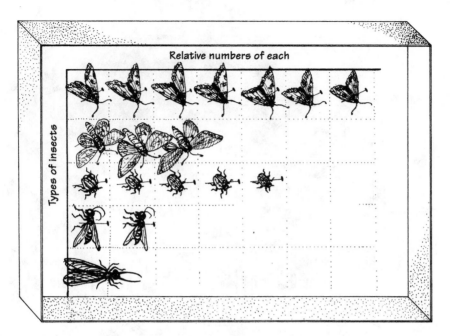

17-2 An insect collection can show not only the types of insects collected but also the relative numbers collected.

18
Fly fisherman's friends
Aquatic insect habitats

Aquatic insects are important members of many ecosystems because they are food for fish and waterfowl. Fly fishermen have studied more aquatic insects than many entomologists, because they use these insects as models for their fishing lures. They create different lures for the different types of fish they are trying to catch.

Do fly fishermen have to change lures when they move from a pond to a stream, or will the same one work in both habitats? Are the aquatic insects found in a stream (running water) different than those found in a pond (standing water)? Do different parts of a pond or a stream contain different types of insects? What are your hypotheses?

MATERIALS

- Aquatic collecting net (can be purchased from a biological supply house or you can use a large, very fine sieve)
- White pan or white bucket
- Forceps
- Heavy gloves
- Rubbing alcohol
- At least eight glass jars or vials, with screw caps that can be closed tightly
- Labels to apply to the jars
- Magnifying glass (optional)

PROCEDURES

Before you go collecting, prepare the jars by filling them about halfway with rubbing alcohol, which will store and preserve the insects.

WARNING: Many aquatic insects can give a bad bite. Do not handle these insects with your bare hands. Use forceps, a sieve, and/or heavy gloves while handling them. Whenever you are collecting near bodies of water, be sure you are accompanied by an adult.

While standing on the shore of a small pond, sweep the net or sieve through the water, especially in areas where vegetation is growing up out of the water. If there are different kinds of vegetation growing out of the water, collect in each different area. In an area where the pond is very shallow, drag the net or sieve across the bottom of the pond (FIG. 18-1). Finally, while wearing gloves, turn over some rocks near the edge of the water and use your forceps to collect any insects clinging to the rocks.

18-1 Collect aquatic insects.

After you've collected from each of these areas, dump the contents of the net or sieve onto the white pan. Using forceps, look through the debris for insects. As you find them, use the forceps to place them in one of the jars containing alcohol. Label each jar "pond #1," "pond #2," etc., as shown (FIG. 18-2). Use a lead pencil to write on the labels, since ink will be dissolved by the alcohol. In your notes, write down which vial was collected from which part of the pond. Continue collecting until you have a variety of insects.

After collecting at the pond, go to a small stream. From the shore, once again collect by sweeping the net or sieve through the water. Then, in a shallow area scrape across the bottom of the stream. There is no need to go into the stream.

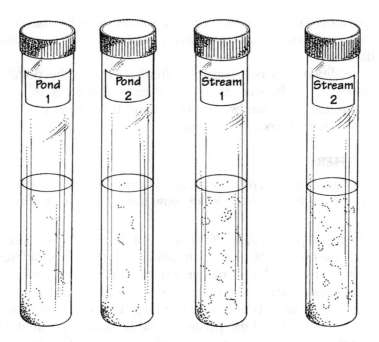

18-2 Store aquatic insects that you've collected in vials containing alcohol.

After collecting in this manner, have your supervisor use a stick to disturb the bottom of the stream while you hold the net in the water downstream to catch insects (and debris) that have been dislodged by the stick. This is called *kicknetting*. Do this for one or two minutes. Finally, put on the gloves and turn some rocks over near the edge of the water and use your forceps to collect any insects attached to the bottom of the rocks.

Once again, as you collect insects, place them in the white pan. Use the forceps to find the insects and put your catch in other alcohol jars that you have labeled, "stream #1", "stream #2", etc.

After you have finished the collecting portion of the project, you can begin to study the insects. Use a magnifying glass, if one is available. Draw sketches of each kind of insect. Then note how many of each were found.

Once you have done this for both collections compare the two and analyze your data. Use your field guide (one designed for aquatic insects would be best) to determine what kinds of insects you found in each habitat. Many of the insects found will be immature forms.

CONCLUSIONS

What kinds of insects did you find in each habitat? Were the same insects collected in the pond and the stream, or did they differ? If they differed, how different were they? Does the ecology of the stream differ enough from the ecology of the pond to cause different insects to inhabit each? If so, what factors are different?

Were there differences between the different parts of the pond? How about different parts of the stream? Was there much difference in the kinds of insects within the pond and within the stream? If so, what factors make them different? What are your conclusions?

GOING FURTHER

- Read more about the life cycles of aquatic insects. Do these insects spend most of their lives in the water? If not, how much of their lives are spent out of water?

- To continue this experiment, see if the speed of the flowing water controls what insects are present. Work with an adult at all times. Do different insects live in the fast section of the stream (the *riffle*) compared with the slower parts of the stream? Use plastic grocery bags to cut five pieces of plastic, 1-inch-wide piece by about 1½ feet long. Tie each piece onto a fist-sized rock. About 1 foot of the plastic should be hanging from the rock. Do this for five rocks. Put the rocks in different parts of a small stream. Place some in areas where there is almost no motion and others of varying water speed. You can do this along the shore, or attach a long string to each and throw the rock in the water, leaving the end of the string on shore so the rock can be retrieved. Return one week later to collect the rocks. Pull the strings in or simply pick up the rocks if they are just off-shore. Observe how many insects are attached to each plastic strip. Which rocks had the most and the least number of insects? Use your field guide to identify the insects.

19

Walking on water
Surface tension, pollution, and aquatic insects

Water has a physical property called *surface tension*. This force is created when water molecules stick together. Very small organisms usually cannot escape this tension and become trapped in water. Some insects, however, depend on the surface tension of water to survive. Water striders, whirligig beetles, and springtails are all examples of insects that live on top of the water and use surface tension to help them travel over the water.

Contaminants in water, such as oil or soap, reduce surface tension. What happens to aquatic insects that normally travel on top of water, when the natural surface tension is destroyed by pollution? What is your hypothesis?

MATERIALS

- Six live insects that live on the water's surface (You can collect these insects, such as waters striders or whirligig beetles, or order them from a biological supply house.)
- Four containers that have the same surface area (You can use milk cartons, cut exactly in half.)
- Measuring cup
- Vegetable oil
- Dish detergent soap

PROCEDURES

Put 2 cups of water in each container. Add three insects to each container. Spend at least ten minutes observing the natural movements of the insects across the water. Carefully observe how the insect contacts the water. Note your observations.

Then, add a few squirts of dish detergent soap to one container and a few tablespoons of oil to the other. Continue to add enough of each contaminant so the surface is completely covered (FIG. 19-1). A thin film covering the entire surface is all you need. Observe the insects in each container.

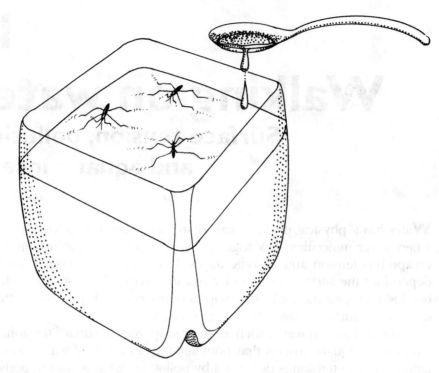

19-1 Test how contaminants affect surface tension.

How is the movement and behavior different than before? Once again observe how the insects contact the water. Note your observations.

CONCLUSIONS

How did the insects move in the unpolluted water? How did they move in each of the contaminants? How does the movement differ? Could the water strider stride, or the whirligig whirl? Did one contaminant have more of an effect than the other? Research what happened to the surface tension and what effect it had on the insects. What are your conclusions?

GOING FURTHER

- Read more about how aquatic insects move through the water.
- Continue this experiment by dipping the legs of a water strider in soap and then placing it in normal water. Can it still skate on the water's surface? What happens after some time passes? How much soap is needed to cause the insect a problem with surface tension?

20
Moby bug
Insects in water

Insects are found in most parts of the world. Most insects are terrestrial, but about 10 percent are aquatic. Where is this 10 percent found? We know insects are found in fresh water, but are they also present in the ocean and in marshes (brackish water)? Are there as many insects in these habitats as in fresh water? What is your hypothesis? You must have access to the ocean, brackish water such as a marsh, and a pond or stream to perform this experiment.

MATERIALS

- Aquatic insect net
- Forceps
- White pan or a white bucket
- Magnifying glass or dissecting microscope
- Three glass jars with secure tops to store collected insects
- Rubbing alcohol

PROCEDURES

Fill the three jars halfway with rubbing alcohol to store and preserve the insects you will collect.

Sweep the aquatic net through the water at the ocean's edge. Do this with your supervisor, in a protected area where the surf isn't rough. Place any organisms you collect in the jar that has been half-filled with alcohol. Mark this jar "ocean."

WARNING: Many aquatic insects can give a bad bite. Do not handle these insects with your bare hands. Use forceps, a sieve, and/or heavy gloves while handling them. Whenever you are collecting near bodies of water, be sure you are accompanied by an adult.

Now collect in a freshwater pond. While standing on the shore, sweep through the water. Do this in areas where vegetation is sticking out of the water. If different types of vegetation are present, sweep in each type of vegetation. Also scrape the bottom of the pond in a shallow area. Finally, put on gloves and turn over some rocks. Use your forceps to pick up any insects you might find. Dump the insects and the debris in a white pan and use your forceps to pick out the insects. Place the insects in the second alcohol jar and mark it "pond."

Make another collection in a *brackish* (partially salty) habitat, like a salt-marsh along a beach. Use the net to sweep the water where vegetation is sticking out. Do this in a few different areas. Dump the collected material into the pan and use your forceps to pick out the insects. Place them in the last alcohol jar, and mark it "brackish."

Once you've finished your collecting, it's time to examine the catch under the microscope or a magnifying glass. Did you collect insects in all three habitats? Count and try to identify the insects collected. Be sure to identify whether the organisms found were insects or other types of arthropods. How did the catch differ in each habitat? Are insects present in all these habitats? Are they more prevalent in one than any other? What are your conclusions?

GOING FURTHER

- Read more about aquatic insects and their habitats.
- Consider also performing the *Fly fisherman's friends* project, along with this one.
- To continue this experiment, collect seaweed that washed up on a beach at the ocean. Inspect the seaweed for organisms. Seaweed often has flies on it. Do these flies live on the seaweed when the weed is underwater? Collect the plant as soon as it washes up on shore and look for the same flies. Are they present or do they arrive later? When people say insects are everywhere, are they really correct?

21
A fishbowl existence
Insects in a food chain

Two of the most important aspects of an organism's environment are the presence of food and predators. A food chain is one way for ecologists to study how an organism lives. How do mosquitoes fit into a food chain? How does the presence or absence of food and predators affect the survival of mosquitoes? How do mosquitoes affect other organisms? What is your hypothesis?

MATERIALS

- Two plant clippings (from an African violet or similar type of plant)
- Liquid house plant fertilizer
- Three ½- gallon clear plastic milk or juice containers, cut in half
- One goldfish
- Aquarium fishnet
- 75 mosquito larvae (purchased from a biological supply house or collected outside)
- Eyedropper without too narrow a tip

PROCEDURES

Put 1 quart of water into two of the containers. Put one drop of liquid plant fertilizer into each container and add one plant clipping to each container. Keep them in direct sunlight for two to three weeks. Add a drop of plant fertilizer every four days to each container. Algae will grow during this time, turning the water green. Once the water is tinted green, remove the plant clippings. The water is ready to be used for the experiment.

Put 1 quart of water into the remaining container. Label this container "mosquitoes only" and put in 25 mosquito larvae. Use the eyedropper or a spoon to transfer the larvae.

Label one of the other two containers, "algae + mosquitoes" and put 25 mosquito larvae into it, using the eyedropper or a spoon.

Label the third container, "algae + mosquitoes + fish," and put 25 mosquito larvae into it, using the eyedropper or the spoon. Use the fishnet to put the goldfish in this container, also.

Leave all three containers in the same room under the same conditions (FIG. 21-1). Every day, count the number of mosquitoes in each container and record this data. Fill in a table similar to TABLE 21-1.

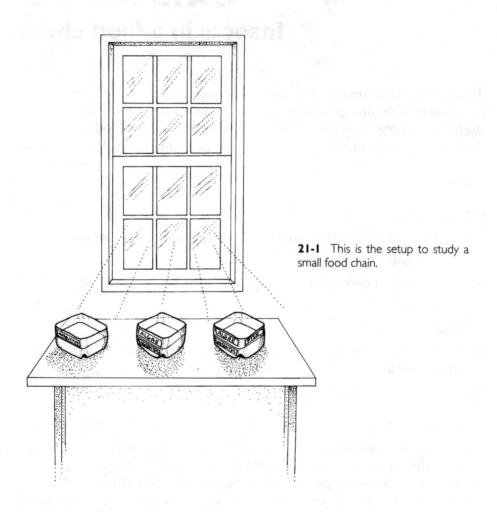

21-1 This is the setup to study a small food chain.

After three days, look closely at a few mosquitoes from each container and record your observations. You might want to draw some sketches of the mosquitoes. Observe and record the overall condition of the mosquitoes, fish, and algae.

Table 21-1   Number of living mosquitoes

	Mosquitoes	Algae & mosquitoes	Algae, mosquitoes & fish
Day 1			
Day 2			
Day 3			

CONCLUSIONS

How does the presence or absence of algae affect the survival of mosquitoes? Can you see a difference between the mosquitoes that came from containers with and without algae? How does the presence or absence of fish affect the mosquito's survival? How did all three components of this food chain interact? Sketch the food chain. What are your conclusions?

When the mosquitoes get to the pupal stage they will emerge as adults within one to three days, so be sure to dispose of them from the water with the eyedropper.

GOING FURTHER

- Read more about insect ecology. Study more complex food chains and food webs that include insects.

- To continue this experiment, change some of the ecological factors and notice how the numbers of mosquitoes over time changes. Try any or all of the following: 1) add some fish food each day while the mosquitoes are present; 2) add some leafy aquatic plants to the container with mosquitoes and fish; or 3) remove the goldfish a few days after the experiment begins. How do these modifications affect the food chain, specifically the survival of the mosquitoes, and why?

Part 3

Insect Lives

Just as fascinating as the total number of insects on our planet is the vast diversity of the lives they lead: from the metamorphosis of a butterfly, which almost every child is familiar with, to the odd reproductive cycles of some aphids that are born pregnant! There are insects that taste with their feet and hear with their legs.

Some insects can only survive by eating one particular species of plant while others will eat almost anything. There are insects that fly thousands of miles and others that live almost their entire lives under a rock.

The experiments in this section will show you how to investigate the lives of many fascinating insects.

22
On and on and on ...
Reproduction and growth of aphids

Insects have extraordinary powers of reproduction. This is one of the reasons they are so successful and so numerous. Since they can produce so many offspring, so quickly, they can recover from disaster very rapidly.

Aphids, also called plant lice, have almost unbelievable reproduction capabilities. They can reproduce without mating, and as unbelievable as it sounds, they are born pregnant! For most of the year, an aphid population is entirely composed of females. Females give birth without ever mating, which is called parthenogenetic reproduction.

There are many insects that reproduce in this manner, but aphids have another unusual capability. Instead of laying eggs like most insects, the female produces live young which are already pregnant with the next generation of offspring. The young aphids begin to feed immediately, and it isn't too long before these young aphids are giving birth.

How many offspring can one female aphid produce in her lifetime? How long does it take to produce all the offspring? What is your hypothesis?

MATERIALS

- A plant infested with aphids (You can find one in a local field or garden, or create your own by placing a bean plant outdoors in a very sunny spot during the summer months, in most parts of the country. It will be naturally infested with aphids within a few weeks.)
- Nylon material
- String
- Forceps or fine tweezers
- Small paintbrush (like one used for painting model planes)
- Magnifying glass

PROCEDURES

This experiment can be done from late spring to early fall. You will select, isolate, and observe one aphid in a colony for two to four weeks. Carefully look on the stem containing the colony for a small individual. It should have no wings. Use a magnifying glass to see it clearly. To isolate this individual, use the brush and/or tweezers to push off all the other aphids nearby. You want this individual to be clear of other aphids in the colony by at least 4 inches in both directions on the stem.

Do not pick up the selected aphid while its beak is inserted into the plant. That would tear off its mouthparts and kill it. If you crush an aphid, it releases a chemical, which causes other aphids to drop off of the stem. You can use this to your advantage while clearing aphids from the stem. If necessary, you can gently pick up an aphid using the brush and place it back on the stem after the others are gone.

Once an individual is isolated, with no neighbors within 4 inches, enclose that part of the plant stem, with the single aphid, in a fine nylon material such as pantyhose, so no other aphids can crawl or fly into that area. Cut a nylon strip 4 to 5 inches wide and wrap it around the stem, so it surrounds the plant loosely. Don't constrict the plant, and leave some room for the aphid. Use string to tie each end of net to the plant stem. Make it tight enough that aphids can't crawl in, but don't crush or break the stem (FIG. 22-1).

Create a similar setup on a different plant, or at least a different part of the same plant, so you'll have two.

Take notes about the date and time you begin the experiment. Return each day to count any new aphids (offspring) within the enclosures. To do this, gently untie and remove the nylon so you can get a clear view of the stem and the aphids. Count the new offspring and then remove them from the enclosure with the brush. The offspring will be smaller than the mother. Once again try not to crush them as they are removed. If the original aphid falls off the stem, carefully place it back on the stem. Replace the netting over the stem after each observation. Do this with each of the two stems.

Continue your observations until offspring are no longer being produced. The original aphid will die shortly thereafter. Keep a record of the date and the number of offspring for each aphid.

CONCLUSIONS

How many offspring did each aphid produce? How long did it take to produce the offspring? How many offspring would be produced in the second generation if they all survived? What are your conclusions?

GOING FURTHER

- Read more about the aphid's life cycle.
- Read more about unusual methods of reproduction such as parthenogenic reproduction and *paedeogenesis* (the young reproduce).

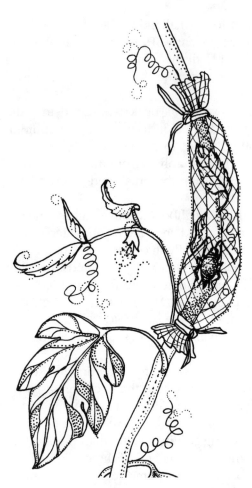

22-1 What is the number of offspring produced by a single female aphid?

- Continue this experiment by determining how an aphid colony affects the health of a plant. Grow four plants, two with aphids and two protected from aphids by netting. Maintain identical growing conditions. Do the plants with the aphids grow as well? What about a plant with just a few aphids (less than 10)? Will even a few aphids hurt a plant's growth?

23
Attractive colors
Can insects see colors?

Insects use all their senses to find what they seek. Flying insects will land when they detect a particular habitat they require, such as a certain type of plant or possibly a pond. There are insects that use sight, smell, sound, and even touch to seek out their food and shelter.

Sight is one of the more common methods of finding something, but is color important in finding what they are looking for? Are some colors more attractive to insects than others? Will certain colors lure insects to land while others won't? What is your hypothesis?

MATERIALS

- Spray paint (yellow, red, blue, green, white, and black)
- Six disposable foil pans (9 inches wide × 12 inches long × 2 inches deep)
- Dish detergent
- Tablespoon measure
- Small sieve or strainer

PROCEDURES

This experiment can be done in late spring through the summer. Spray the inside of each pan a different color. Let the paint completely dry. Fill each pan with ½ inch soapy water. Use at least 1 tablespoon of soap per pan, but don't make it so soapy that you can't see the paint color through the water. The soap traps the insects.

Set the pans outside in middle of a field. If the vegetation is high, put the pans on top of boxes, so they are above the level of the vegetation (FIG. 23-1).

Every day or two, collect the insects in each pan. Scoop the insects out with a sieve or fine strainer. You will have to refill the pans with soapy water every few days. Continue this procedure for about two weeks. Count the number of insects caught in each pan and use your field guide to identify the kinds of insects caught. Take notes during each observation.

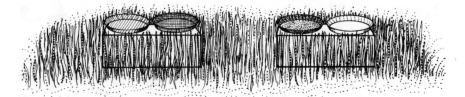

23-1 Investigate whether insects can see color.

CONCLUSIONS

Do you get a different number of insects in each pan? Do you get different kinds of insects in each pan? Does any one color seem more attractive to insects? Does any one color seem less attractive? Does color play a role in attracting insects? Was your hypothesis correct?

GOING FURTHER

- Read more about how insects see. Do all insects see in the same way? What do the pans look like to an insect?

- To continue this experiment, use different shades of the color found to be the most attractive to the insects. Spray different pans different shades of this color. Can insects distinguish between certain shades? Do they find a particular shade more alluring?

24
Night flyers
How insects find their way at night

Many insects perceive their world by comparing what their right side senses with what their left side senses. When ants are on a chemical trail they don't walk in a straight line. They move right and then left and then right, ultimately staying on the trail, but constantly swerving back and forth. This is because they are comparing the odors that their right antenna is sensing compared to the left. They turn to the side sensing the strongest smell.

Most moths use the light of the moon to guide them. Do they follow the moonlight much like ants follow a trail?

MATERIALS

- Two large, live moths (You can collect them at night near a light.)
- Flashlight
- Darkened room
- Tweezers
- Stick-on labels (like those used for adhering to an envelope)
- Insect collecting net

PROCEDURES

Use your net to capture a large moth around a light at night. The bigger the moth, the better. Once you have the moth in the net, bring it into a dark room. Put the flashlight in the middle of a room, standing on its end, pointing up. Have all the other lights in the room turned off. Release the moth in the room. What does it do? Observe the moth's behavior for about five minutes. Recapture the moth with the net and record your observations (FIG. 24-1).

Cut a small circle about the size of the moth's eye out of the label. This will act like an eyepatch.

Now, carefully hold the moth in your fingers while it is still in the net. Try not to damage its wings. Turn the net inside out, so the insect's head is

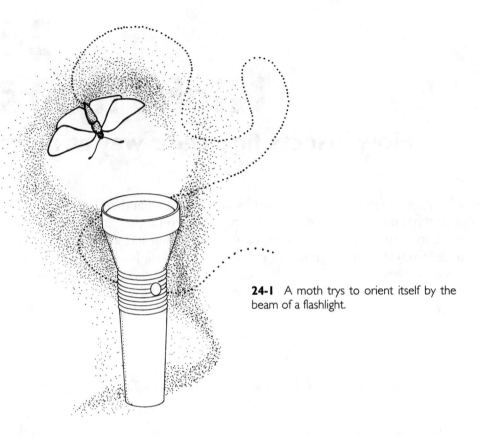

24-1 A moth trys to orient itself by the beam of a flashlight.

visible through the net's opening. Using the tweezers, have a partner carefully place the small eyepatch on one of the moth's eyes.

Turn the lights back off and release the moth again in the dark room with the flashlight on. Once again, observe its behavior for five minutes. How does it differ from its earlier behavior? Recapture the moth once again. Take notes about what you observed.

After you are finished observing the first moth, catch a a second moth. Instead of placing the patch over an eye, place it on a spot on its thorax (on its back, where the wings attach). This moth is the *control* moth, to see if it is the patch that causes a change in behavior, instead of covering an eye. How does this moth react? Record your observations.

CONCLUSIONS

How did the flight of the control moth compare with the flight of the moth with one eye covered? Was the moth able to navigate with only one working eye? If not, why not? What happened to its flight path and why? Was the control moth's flight normal? What does this tell you about the experiment? Was your hypothesis correct?

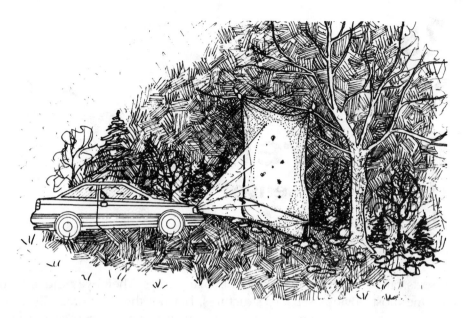

24-2 Collect night-flying insects using a sheet and car headlights.

GOING FURTHER

- Read more about insect flight, especially night flight.
- Create a collection of night-flying insects using a setup as shown (FIG. 24-2). Numerous insects will be captured in the sheet's trough.
- To continue this experiment, use the same setup but swing the flashlight back and forth. What do the moths do? Can the normal moth or the others follow the light?

25
Your taste is where?
How insects sense the "taste"

Insects can sense their environment in many ways. Their eyes and antennae are the most obvious sensory structures, but not the only ones. By careful observation can you find other sensory structures on insects? We'll use a fly, which is a good example of an insect that uses odd parts of its body to sense the environment. What part of a fly's body is used to taste its food? What happens when they sense food? What are your hypotheses?

MATERIALS

- Two live adult blowflies (These can be purchased from a biological supply house. They usually come in the pupal form with adults emerging within one week.)
- A refrigerator to slow the flies down
- Rubber cement
- Applicator sticks, such as coffee stirrers or popsicle sticks
- Forceps or tweezers
- Cup
- Teaspoon
- Two saucers

PROCEDURES

First, the flies must be immobilized without harming them. Place the container holding the flies in a refrigerator for about ten minutes to slow them down. Once the flies are no longer moving, open the container and gently take out one fly with the forceps. Put the others back in the refrigerator. Put

25-1 This is the setup to test what part of a fly's body "tastes" food.

a drop of rubber cement directly on the back of the fly, between its wings. Place another drop of glue at the end of an applicator stick. Touch the two globs of glue together so the fly is attached to the stick and hanging down as you see in the illustration (FIG. 25-1).

Set the stick and fly in the cup in an upright position so you don't harm the fly. Repeat this process with the other fly and place it in the cup, also. After a few minutes, the flies will recover from the cold and try to fly.

You want the flies to be hungry, not thirsty. Let them drink water before beginning the experiment. Pick up and hold one of the sticks. Dip the fly's mouthparts as you see in the illustration, so it just barely touches the water (FIG. 25-1). You'll notice its mouth (*proboscis*) lapping up the water. Let it drink as much as it wants. When it is no longer drinking, put the stick back in the cup and do the same with the other stick and fly.

Leave both flies in the cup for 10 minutes. While waiting, draw a sketch of what the mouthparts looked like when the flies were drinking the water.

Now find out how an insect tastes food. Create a sugar solution by mixing 3 teaspoons of sugar in 3 or 4 tablespoons of water. Pour this solution into a saucer. Take one of the flies and dip different parts of the fly's body into the sugar water solution. First, just barely touch the tips of the fly's legs (tarsi) into the water. Does its proboscis drop to feed? Now try the top of its head above its eyes. Did the proboscis drop? Try the wings, and the tip of its abdomen. How about the proboscis itself? Does it extend when it touches the water?

Repeat the entire procedure with the second fly. Are the results the same? Write down what happened for each body part.

CONCLUSIONS

From your observations, can you tell which parts of the fly's body can taste? Can the fly taste with more than one part of its body? Was your hypothesis correct?

GOING FURTHER

- Read more about the sensory structures of insects. How do they taste, hear, touch, smell? Do all insects sense the environment the same way?

- To continue this experiment, make up various sugar water concentrations. (See "As sweet as can be" for a good range of solutions). Touch the fly (on the stick) into different concentrations and make notes on the movements of their mouthparts. Can the fly taste them all, or only a few?

26
Picky eaters
Food selection

There are hundreds of thousands of insects that eat plants. If farmers had to cope with all of these plant eaters, they would probably never be able to grow any food. If an insect eats plants originally intended for us to eat, the insect is considered a pest. While some insect pests eat almost any kind of plant, luckily, most only eat one type of plant. This makes it less likely that numerous different types of insects will eat our crops, and it is easier to control those that do eat a particular crop.

This experiment investigates the feeding preferences of a typical insect pest. What is the favorite host plant of the tobacco hornworm caterpillar (other than tobacco!)? Will they eat other types of foods if they have to? State your hypothesis and proceed with the project.

MATERIALS

- Two tomato plants at least 6 inches high (You can purchase these in the spring at a garden center or a supermarket.)
- Two bean plants at least 6 inches high (You can purchase these in the spring at garden center.)
- Four tobacco hornworm caterpillars (These can be ordered from a biological supply house. If you have a garden, you might be able to capture them yourself.)
- Plastic sheet, 12 inches wide × 8 feet long
- Plastic waterproof tape
- Four stakes, 12 to 16 inches long
- Hammer
- Newspaper
- Garden shovel

PROCEDURES

Build an outdoor enclosure to protect the project. Hammer four stakes to form the corners of a 2-x-2 foot square. Attach one end of the plastic sheet to one stake with tape. Wind the plastic around the other stakes to form a fence-like enclosure and then tape or tack its end to the original stake (FIG. 26-1).

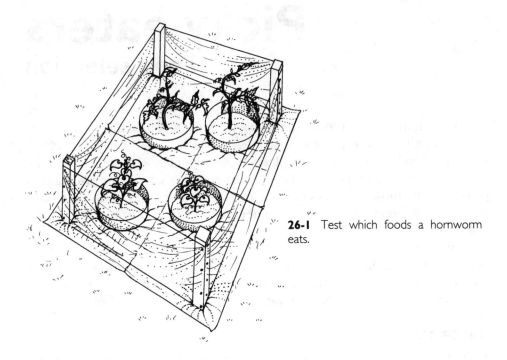

26-1 Test which foods a hornworm eats.

With a garden shovel dig four holes for the plant pots. You want the top of the pot to be the same level as the ground. Insert the pots into the holes. Lay newspaper on the ground all around the pots so the caterpillars have no access to the grass or other growth in the enclosure.

Put the four caterpillars inside the enclosure. Place the hornworms on the newspaper between the two types of plants. Note the time you begin the project. Return every hour for the first several hours on the first day to see where the caterpillars are and what they are feeding on. Be sure to take notes of your observations. Once they have selected a plant to feed on, observe them once a day. Continue writing down your observations.

CONCLUSIONS

Do they eat both plants at first? Do they prefer one to the other? If they prefer one type of plant to the other, what happens when the preferred plant is eaten? Will they eat the other? Research why they eat and what they eat. What are your conclusions about the hornworms' feeding habits?

GOING FURTHER

- Read more about how insects distinguish between one plant and another. If they are picky about what they eat, how can they tell what they are eating? Can they tell if they like a plant before they eat it?

- Continue this experiment, but use caterpillars that you've found. Keep two piles of food in the enclosure with the caterpillar. The first pile should be the same type of plant leaves the caterpillar was eating when you found it. The second pile of leaves should come from a different type of plant. Try removing the original food plant and see if the caterpillar eats the other leaves.

- You can also continue the original experiment but use other types of plants (potato, strawberry, different strains of tomato, pumpkin, or squash). Are there certain families of plants that the caterpillars eat and others they won't eat?

27
Living in a leaf
Insects that make their
homes in plants

Insects often live in close association with plants. Some insects with the most interesting relationships are *gall* producers, *leaf miners*, and *leaf rollers* (FIG. 27-1).

Galls are deformities in a plant. Some look like small, odd growths protruding from leaves or stems, while others are large, round growths that almost look as if they belong on the plant. Galls, however, are not normal plant growths. They are caused by plant diseases, nematodes, or very often, insects. The insects produce a substance that causes the plant to produce growths (the galls), which the insects use as a home for protection.

Other types of insects create leaf mines or tunnels within stems and leaves. An insect lays an egg within the leaf. When the immature insect emerges from the egg, it feeds within the leaf creating small mines (tunnels). As the insect grows, the mine gets wider. The insect continues its life cycle within the leaf until the adult burrows its way out.

The leaf roller is an insect that uses a leaf for protection as it matures. It rolls the leaf up into a tight cylinder around its body.

How common are these insect-created plant structures? How many different ones can you find? How do insects use these structures? Is the plant harmed by this intrusion? What are your hypotheses?

MATERIALS
- Good-quality magnifying glass or a dissecting microscope
- Scalpel or a fine blade
- Forceps
- Plastic baggies for collecting
- Small jars or vials with covers
- Rubbing alcohol

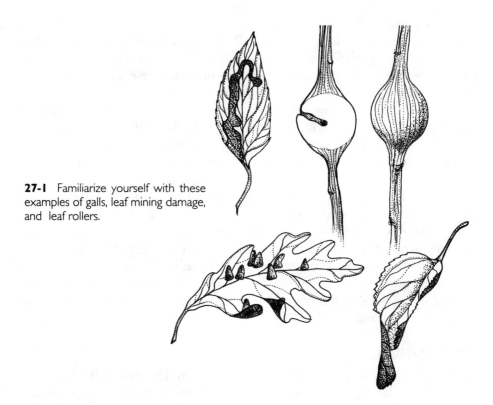

27-1 Familiarize yourself with these examples of galls, leaf mining damage, and leaf rollers.

PROCEDURES

In the late spring to early fall, look for plants containing galls, leaf mining, and leaf rolling damage. Look on the leaves and stems of shrubs, trees, and other perennial plants for these structures. A walk in the woods would probably have the best results. See your field guide for examples of these types of damage (FIG. 27-1). Try to collect at least 10 types. Cut off the small portion of the plant containing the damage and place it in a plastic bag.

Take the specimens home or to school and study them under a dissecting microscope or a high-powered magnifying glass. Galls are often large and easy to study. Leaf mining damage is easy to see. Look for the gradual widening of the tunnel on the leaf surface. Leaf rollers are also easy to study. Before dissecting the damage, take notes and make sketches of your observations.

Once you have studied the external structures, dissect each one, and study the internal structure of the plant damage, searching for the insects that caused the damage. The insect inhabitants will be much harder to find than the damage they caused. Cut galls open with a scalpel or a sharp knife.

Look for insect larvae. If you don't find the insect at first, take notes and make a sketch of the inside of the gall. Then, proceed to carefully cut the gall into smaller pieces in search of the inhabitant. If you find the insect, try to identify it using the gall and the insect. Place the insect in a vial containing alcohol to preserve it.

To study the leaf roller, unroll the leaf using forceps and the scalpel. It's probably held together with a glue or a web. Tease the holding material apart to unravel the leaf. What is inside? Try to identify the insect. Use the insect and the structure of the rolled leaf to identify it. Place the insect in a vial containing alcohol.

Leaf miners are usually very small and may be hard if not impossible to locate. Use the microscope or magnifying glass to look at the end of the widest portion of the mine. Is there a small hole at the end? If so, this is the emergence hole where the adult insect left the leaf. The hole may be on the top, bottom, or even at the edge of the leaf. If possible, find a leaf that does not have a hole, meaning the insect is still inside. With the dissecting scope, look at the end of the widest part of the mine for the insect. Take notes and make sketches of all your observations.

CONCLUSIONS

Are these insect and plant relationships common? Did you find many different types of damage? Did you find many of one kind of damage? How do the insects appear to be using the plants to their benefit? How harmful is the damage to the plant? What would happen if the plant died with the insects in it? What are your conclusions?

GOING FURTHER

- Read more about gall producers, leaf miners, leaf rollers, and similar types of insects. Study their life cycle. How do they select the host plant? What stimulates the plant to produce the gall?

- Continue this experiment by finding a large gall or rolled leaf, and place a very fine net over it. Secure the net tightly over and around the leaf or stem. Do this to a few different types of galls or leaf rolls. Check the net carefully every few days. The easiest way to see if the insect has emerged is to check the plant first for holes or other changes. If it appears as if something has emerged, look carefully for the insect in the net.

28

Overpopulation: insect style
Population growth

Some insects reproduce very quickly, while others take many years to produce a single generation. Ecologists and entomologists must understand the population growth of an insect to understand how the species survives and determine how it fits into the ecology of a habitat. Studying population growth dynamics is an important part of understanding the biology of an insect. This experiment involves no live insects.

Can you determine mathematically how long it takes for a single female insect to generate a population of 250,000 insects? To resolve this problem you need specific information about the insect in question. The estimated generation time, birth rate, and mortality (death rate) for the common fruitfly is given below. After calculating the population, determine what happens when you figure into the calculation the number of insects that don't survive (*mortality factors*).

What do you hypothesize about the length of time it would take to reach 250,000 fruitflies if there were no deaths? How dramatically would differing amounts of mortality affect how long it took to reach 250,000? Do you think the population growth rate would differ depending on the stage in the insect's life cycle that the mortality occurs? For example, does the population reach 250,000 individuals in the same amount of time if 10 percent of the eggs die and 50 percent of the pupae die, or if the opposite were true?

MATERIALS

- Calculator
- Graph paper

PROCEDURES

A pair of fruitflies can produce a new generation every fifteen days. Each female can lay 100 eggs (assume one-half of which will be male). Under ideal conditions (all the offspring survive to reproduce), how long will it take to reach a population of 250,000 fruitflies? Graph this population increase on a chart (TABLE 28-1).

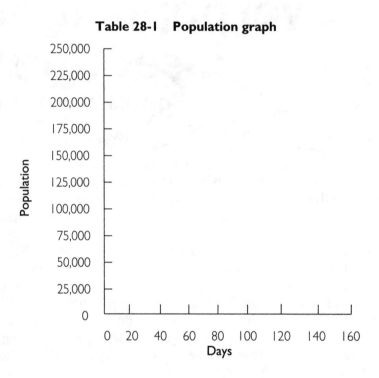

Table 28-1   Population graph

After you calculate the numbers under ideal conditions, be more realistic. Vast numbers of insects don't survive to reproduce. Some are eaten by predators, some die of disease, and some will succumb to the environment. Make the following assumptions about mortality rates. Assume that 30 percent of the eggs are destroyed by predators, 20 percent of the larvae die from harsh weather conditions, and 10 percent of the pupal stage never emerge as adults due to being physically damaged by other animals.

How long would it take this population to reach the 250,000 mark? Graph these results on the same graph paper you used earlier. What if the egg mortality increased by 10 percent (to 40 percent)? Graph this growth curve. Finally, what if the pupae mortality increased by 10 percent (to 20 percent)? Graph these results on the same paper also.

CONCLUSIONS

Was your hypothesis about reaching 250,000 individuals correct? Is mortality important in slowing population growth? Does mortality of a particular stage have a more dramatic effect on the overall population than another stage? If so, why? What are your conclusions?

GOING FURTHER

- Read more about the population dynamics of insects. How important are insect predators, disease, and environmental factors in controlling insect populations?

- Create a hypothetical "insect population growth doomsday chart." What if there were no predators or other factors to control an insect's reproductive capabilities? How long before the world would be overrun with this insect? Consider entering the insect's weight into the calculation.

- To continue this experiment, research another insect's population dynamics. Find out the duration of an insect's life cycle, how many offspring it can produce, and the approximate number of offspring that are female. Perform the same calculations as above, to see how long before this insect's population would reach 250,000 under ideal conditions. Find out the expected mortality rates and figure these in to your calculations. How do they compare with the fruitfly?

29
Living a complete life
Insect life cycles

As insects grow, their form usually changes. This process is called *metamorphosis*. There are three types of insect metamorphosis. *Ametabolous* insects don't change their general body form at all. *Hemimetabolous* insects undergo incomplete metamorphosis, going from the egg to an immature stage called a *nymph*, to the adult. *Holometabolous* insects undergo complete metamorphosis, changing from the egg to the immature larvae, to still another immature stage called a *pupa*, and then finally to the adult (FIG. 29-1).

Compare the life cycles of insects that undergo each of these types of metamorphoses. How does the body form differ from young to old in each type of life cycle? What structural differences do you see between each stage of each type? What structures stay the same? Are the changes gradual or dramatic? What are the advantages and disadvantages of each kind of life cycle? What are your hypotheses?

MATERIALS

- Preserved specimens of each stage of development of a silverfish or other ametabolous insect (Your school may already have collections of specimens, or they can be purchased from a biological supply house.)
- Preserved specimens of each life stage of a cricket or other hemimetabolous insect (You can purchase crickets from most pet stores. Use a killing jar before examining the insects. Select as many different sizes as possible. They are also available at bait stores or biological supply houses.)
- Preserved specimens of each life stage of a butterfly, moth, beetle, or other holometabolous insect. (They can be purchased from a biological supply house, or your school may already have specimens.)
- Drawing paper
- Dissecting microscope or magnifying glass

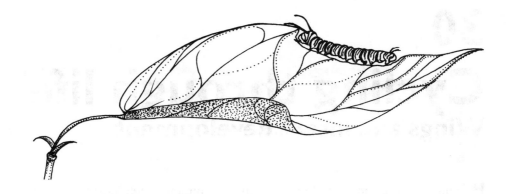

29-1 A single type of insect can have many habitats.

PROCEDURES

This experiment can be done at any time of the year. Perform the following procedures for each of the four kinds of metamorphoses. Look at each stage of the insects' development. Use a microscope or a magnifying glass to closely observe the body form and structures. Draw each insect stage and take notes. Determine what body regions or structures remain the same and which change from stage to stage.

Besides general form, look carefully at each insect's mouthparts. See which structures gradually changed and which changed dramatically from stage to stage. Also look carefully at each stage's wings (if they have them). How do they change? Take notes of your observations.

CONCLUSIONS

What are the basic differences and similarities between the different stages of development within one kind of life cycle? Which structures change the most and which the least? Which structures change the slowest and which the most rapidly? Do some structures not change at all? After studying stages within each type of life cycle, study the differences and similarities between the life cycles. What are the advantages and disadvantages of each? What are your conclusions?

GOING FURTHER

- Read more about insect life cycles. Which are considered more advanced than others and why? Investigate the insects' various feeding habits and their habitats at different stages of their lives.

- To continue this experiment look at other types of holometabolous insects. Do all holometabolous insects have the same life cycle pattern, or are there differences even between insects with this type of development?

30
Cycling through life
Wings and insect development

Hemimetabolous insects (those with incomplete metamorphosis) and holometabolous insects (those with complete metamorphosis) usually have wings. How, when, and where do wings develop in the life cycle of these two types of insects? What is your hypothesis?

MATERIALS

- A small, immature cricket or other insect with incomplete metamorphosis (available from a pet or bait store)
- Mealworm or other insect with complete metamorphosis (available from a pet store)
- Two quart-size canning jars
- Nylon material to cover jars
- Two rubber bands to hold nylon material on jars
- Cotton balls
- Wheat bran
- Oats
- Small plastic sandwich bags

PROCEDURES

Observe each insect's form. As adults, both of these insects will have two sets of wings. Are wings present on either immature insect? Can you find developing wings? Take notes and draw sketches of both insects. Also note the date you started the experiment. You will rear these insects and watch the development of their wings.

Put wheat bran in one jar so it is about half-filled. Moisten with water about one-fifth of the bran (wet but not soaked) and put the mealworm inside. Cover the jar with the nylon material and a rubber band (FIG. 30-1). You'll have to replace the wheat bran every two to three weeks. Remoisten the bran if it dries out.

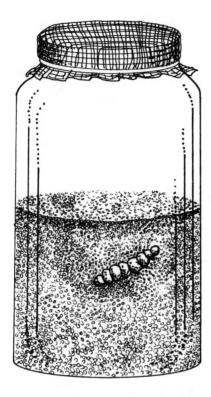

30-1 This is the setup to rear mealworms.

Put about ½ inch of oats on the bottom of the other jar. Put a wet cotton ball in the sandwich bag, and put the open sandwich bag on top of the oats. This is the cricket's water supply. Put the cricket inside the jar and close it with the nylon material and a rubber band (FIG. 30-2). You'll have to re-moisten the cotton every two to four days and replace the oats about once a week.

Look at each insect carefully every two or three days, checking for developing wings. Enter the date in your notes and draw a sketch of the insect. Continue the experiment until the wings on both insects are fully developed. Use your field guide to see a mature adult.

CONCLUSIONS

How did the wings develop on each of the insects? When did they first become visible? When were they fully developed? Where did the wings begin to develop? Although they look very different, are they attached to the same part of each insect's body? Did the wings develop the same way in both insects? What might be advantages and disadvantages of each type of wing development? What are your conclusions?

30-2 This is the setup to rear crickets.

GOING FURTHER

- Read more about insect development. Can you identify the type of metamorphosis an insect undergoes by looking at the immature insect's wings, or lack of them?

- To continue this project, collect some immature insects in the field, and hypothesize their type of metamorphosis based on what they look like. Prove or disprove your hypothesis by either identifying them in your field guide or rearing them to maturity.

31
Getting through the winter
Surviving the cold

When winter approaches, many of the insects we see all summer disappear. What happens to insects in the winter? Some have prepared for the cold by digging down into the soil or leaf litter which protects them from freezing. Some insects do what the robins do; they head south for the winter. But some insects follow the example of the bear; they "sleep" through the winter. Bears hibernate, but insects go through *diapause*, which is something like a suspended animation. Some of these insects produce an "antifreeze" in their bloodstream so they won't freeze during diapause.

Can you find insects in the winter? Is there a certain temperature that brings insects out of diapause?

MATERIALS

- Thermometer (–5°F to 65°F range)
- Insect collecting net
- Insect killing jar

PROCEDURES

Go insect collecting on several occasions during the winter months. Collect on cold winter days and also on milder days in the winter when the temperature is considerably above average. A warm spell of a couple of days in the winter would be the best time.

Look in both types of weather in the same locations for insects. Look near your house and other buildings around the foundation. Use a stick to rummage under leaf litter in the woods, near streams and around ponds. Walk through a field, meadow, or a lawn. Check other areas such as barns, doghouses, woodpiles, and rocks in sunlight. Can you find insects? If you find them, are they active or motionless?

If you find them, take notes about where you observed them and the conditions. Note the date, temperature, and general weather at the time of the insect sighting. Was it sunny and windless or in the shade and windy? What was the insect doing? Collect the insect and continue your research.

When you return with the insects, count how many were collected on each day and use your insect field guide to identify them. Perform this procedure for both the cold-day collection and the warm-day collection.

CONCLUSIONS

How many insects did you collect on the cold versus the warm days? If any insects were caught what was the temperature at that time? Does there seem to be a certain temperature that must be reached in your area for insects to appear? Was your hypothesis correct? What are your conclusions?

GOING FURTHER

- Read more about how insects survive through winter. Which insects use an antifreeze in their blood? Which ones migrate south?

- You can continue this experiment by digging a few inches into leaf litter to find a hibernating insect. It might appear dead or move slightly. Place it in a jar under an incandescent lamp to heat it up. Is heat alone enough to bring an insect out of hibernation or are other factors involved?

Part 4

Insect Form and Function

The study of an organism's form is called *morphology*. By form, we mean the overall structure of an organism. What are the parts and how are they put together? The study of how these parts work or function is called *physiology*.

The basic form of insects is one of the reasons they are such successful organisms. They are found almost everywhere. Their form can protect them from the weather and from predators. It permits them to travel great distances, to eat many types of food, and to breathe and retain moisture.

Wings have helped insects disperse throughout the world and given them access to foods and habitats not available to other animals. Even though many insects look so different from other insects, they all have the same form. It has simply been adapted for survival in different habitats.

Insects have their skeleton on the outside, called an *exoskeleton*. This gives them great strength, compared to animals with internal skeletons. A hollow tube is stronger than a solid tube of the same size. Insects are great examples of how this engineering technique is used by organisms. Their skeletons are like hollow tubes compared to human skeletons, which are solid bones. This makes the insect, ounce for ounce, much stronger than humans.

32
Breathing tubes
Respiration in aquatic insects

Aquatic insects use many different unique ways to obtain oxygen to survive. Some absorb oxygen from the water through their skin. Others carry a bubble of air around with them, while still others use a breathing tube. Insects that use breathing tubes periodically surface and stick the end of this tube out of the water and into the air. Rat-tailed maggots, giant water bugs, water scorpions, and mosquitoes all use a breathing tube.

How do mosquito larvae get oxygen while in the water? Do they absorb it directly from the water or get it from the air? What is your hypothesis?

MATERIALS

- Goldfish bowl
- Five or more mosquito larvae (They can be collected in warm weather from a small pool or a container filled with water and left outside for a few weeks. They can also be purchased from a biological supply house.)
- Eyedropper without a narrow tip
- Dry ice (**CAUTION!** Always use tongs and gloves when handling dry ice. It is very cold and will "burn" your skin if you touch it!)
- Heavy duty foil baking pan (about 9 inches wide × 12 inches long × 2 inches high)
- Knife with pointed tip

PROCEDURES

This experiment can be done at any time of the year. Fill the goldfish bowl halfway with water. Put the mosquito larvae in the goldfish bowl, using the eyedropper or a spoon. Watch their behavior for 10 minutes and note your observations. What do they do in the water? How do they move? Where do they rest? Where do they swim: at the bottom or at the top?

Cut a 2-inch-diameter hole in a foil pan. Set the pan on top of the fishbowl, so the hole is over the water. Using tongs, place the dry ice in the pan but not over the hole (FIG. 32-1).

As the dry ice melts, it turns into gaseous carbon dioxide, which is heav-

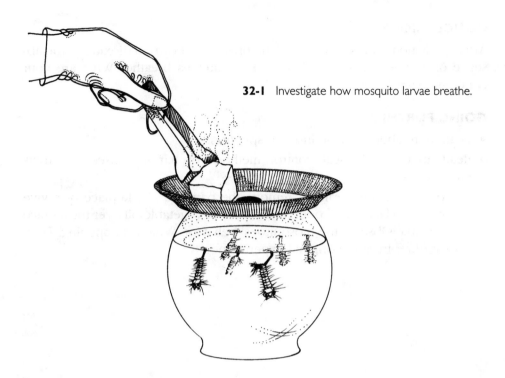

32-1 Investigate how mosquito larvae breathe.

ier than air. It falls through the hole onto the surface of the water and is trapped in the bowl. This puts a layer of carbon dioxide over the top of the water (FIG. 32-2). Watch the mosquitoes for one hour. Observe and record their movements. What happens?

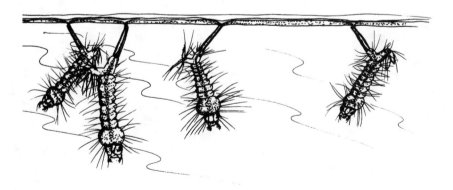

32-2 Observe the mosquito larvae.

CONCLUSIONS

Are the reactions you see results of the presence of carbon dioxide or the absence of another substance? How do mosquitoes breathe? What are your conclusions?

GOING FURTHER

- Read more about aquatic insect respiration.
- Read about mechanical control methods of harmful insects such as mosquitoes.
- To continue this experiment remove the pan and ice. Replace or revive the mosquito larvae and pour a thin layer of vegetable oil over the surface of the water. Observe the mosquitoes' behavior. What is happening? How does it differ from the original experiment?

33
Trekkers
Insect muscles and moving

Insects can travel tremendous distances. Monarch butterflies annually migrate thousands of miles, from Canada to Mexico. Locusts can travel across the width of Africa, while other insects might not change their location their entire lives. Some insects that can fly rarely do. How far do most of the insects in a local field travel? How quickly do they travel? What is your hypothesis?

MATERIALS

- Insect collecting net
- Talcum powder
- Stake or marker
- Yardstick
- Black pan

PROCEDURES

This experiment should be done in late spring to late summer and should be started in the morning, but after any dew has dried. The vegetation must be completely dry. Find a grassy meadow or field that has not been mowed for a few weeks. The vegetation should be ankle to knee high for best results. You will make a large sweep net collection of the insects in a meadow or a field, and release them to be recaptured at a later time.

Sweep the field or meadow with the net to collect insects living in the vegetation. To sweep, move the net rapidly back and forth in front of you while you slowly walk through the meadow. Walk and sweep for about ten minutes. To stop, flip the net closed by twisting the net opening downwards. This folds the net over the net rim and traps the insects inside. All the insects will be in the bottom of the net. You should have more than 100 insects for best results. If not, continue sweeping.

To mark the insects so you can find them again later, open the net and quickly dust the contents with talcum powder. Close the net and gently shake the bundle to mark all the insects. Repeat this procedure a few times to be sure the insects are well marked.

Once they are marked, release them from the net in the center of the field. Dump them all in one spot. Mark the spot where they were released with the stake, so you can measure from that point. Record the time of the release.

You will now begin the recapture part of the experiment. Perform the following steps 30 minutes after the release of the insects.

Stand at the stake where the insects were released. Take two large strides away from the post in any direction. Sweep the area by moving your net side to side as far as possible. Look in the net for white, dust-covered insects. It might be easier to find the marked insects by dumping them into a black pan. If you find any, put a "+" sign on a chart (TABLE 33-1) under that stride distance and time. Now dump out the insects exactly where you found them. You will try to recapture them again later.

Table 33-1   Time from release

Strides	Thirty minutes	One hour	Three hours	Eight hours	One day
2					
4					
6					
8					
10					
20					

Take two more strides out from the post. Be sure to keep the length of your stride constant. Once again, sweep the area, record the presence of dusted insects in the chart, and release the insects at that spot. Take another two strides (you're now six strides from the release point), sweep, check for dusted insects, and release (FIG. 33-1).

Continue this procedure until you have collected no dusted insects for two consecutive sweeps. If very few insects were found, perform the same procedure, but walk away from the marker in another direction. Add the results to the chart.

Wait thirty minutes and perform the same procedure. As you find insects,

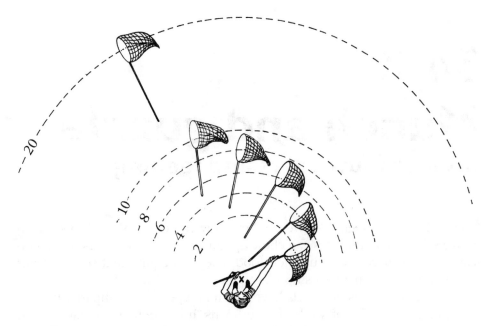

33-1 Take two strides away from where you released the insects.

mark the chart with "+" marks under the sixty minute column. Continue this every thirty minutes for a few hours. You can skip a few intervals and come back at a later time to complete the data collection. Come back about twenty-four hours after the release time and perform one last sweep. You'll have to look carefully for the remaining powder. Be sure to write down what happens.

Use a yardstick to figure out how many feet are in one of your strides, so you can figure out how far the insects traveled, in feet per hour.

CONCLUSIONS

Analyze the data on your chart. How far did the insects travel? How fast could they travel, in feet per hour? Do most insects travel great distances or stay in one spot in the field? What are your conclusions?

GOING FURTHER

- Read more about the fascinating ways some insects travel.
- Continue this experiment by performing the procedure once again, but place the collected insects in a killing jar and identify them with your field guide. Do certain kinds of insects travel farther than others?

34
Munch and guzzle
Insect mouthparts and feeding

Insects don't have teeth like we do. Yet many can eat very hard foods such as live wood! Grasshoppers can chew up grasses, and caterpillars munch on leaves. Other insects suck up their food, like a mosquito that sucks up our blood or an aphid that sucks up plant sap.

Do different types of insects have different types of mouthparts? If there are insects with different kinds of mouthparts, how are they specialized and how do they work? What is your hypothesis?

MATERIALS

- A live chewing insect such as a cricket or grasshopper (Capture your own or buy it at a pet store.)
- A live sucking insect such as a true bug (order Hemiptera: like a milkweed bug, squash bug, or stink bug) or an aphid (order Homoptera) (Capture your own or buy milkweed bugs from a biological supply house.)
- A live butterfly or moth (order Lepidoptera) (Capture your own or buy them from a biological supply house.)
- Dissecting microscope or magnifying lens
- Drawing paper
- Collecting net
- Killing jar

PROCEDURES

Observe the insects while they are feeding. This can be done in the wild or in a container to ensure they don't get away. The insects listed above will usually remain in one place while feeding, long enough for you to observe them. You might need a magnifying lens for the smaller insects.

First, observe the chewing insect. If you are observing a captured or purchased cricket, feed it oats and watch it eat. Next, observe the sucking insect as it feeds. Don't handle these insects, since some can bite. Use your magnifying lens to look closely at its mouthparts as it feeds. Aphids feed on the stem, while many bugs feed directly on leaves.

Finally, observe a butterfly feeding on a flower. You might be able to observe one in the wild. If you prefer, use a collecting net to capture one. Collect the flower it was feeding on at the time you caught it and place both in a jar. Carefully observe as it feeds on the flower.

As you make your observations for all three types of insects, take detailed notes and draw sketches. What mouthparts do you see? What are the mouthparts doing? Also notice how the head moves.

Once you have completed all your observations, place all the insects in a killing jar. After about an hour remove them and study each insect's mouthparts under the dissecting scope. Draw sketches. Study the various parts of each. Refer to your field guide for assistance.

CONCLUSIONS

Analyze your data. First, review your notes to see how the insects' feeding habits differed. Then look at your notes to see how the mouthparts differ and how they are similar. Do insects with different feeding habits have dif-

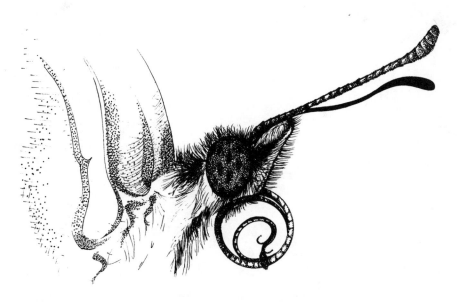

34-1 The butterfly's mouthparts.

ferent types of mouthparts? How has the form of an insect's mouthparts adapted to its function (FIG. 34-1)? What conclusions can you draw?

GOING FURTHER

- Read more about insect mouthparts and feeding behavior. Do all insects have mouthparts? Do all adult insects eat?
- Compare the variety of insect mouthparts with another class of organism such as mammals. Which has greater diversity?
- To continue this experiment, make a collection of insects representing different types of mouthparts.

35
Breathing holes
How terrestrial insects breathe

We breathe air into our lungs, where blood picks up oxygen and carries it through our circulatory system to every cell in our body. Insects don't have lungs nor do they have a circulatory system that carries oxygen to their cells. Without lungs or oxygen carrying blood, how does an insect's cells get oxygen to survive?

What they do have is a system of internal tubes that brings air from the outside directly to all their cells. Openings to the outside, called *spiracles*, let air into a *tracheal* system. The tracheal system carries oxygen to all the cells in the body.

What happens if the spiracles get blocked by pollutants? What materials can block these openings? Can an insect survive long without air? What happens if the spiracles are reopened? Determine your hypothesis and proceed with the experiment.

MATERIALS

- Four large mealworms (from a pet store)
- 1-cup container
- Dish detergent
- Petroleum jelly
- Vegetable oil
- Tablespoon measure
- Forceps
- Four small foil pans

PROCEDURES

This experiment can be done at any time of the year. You will block the spiracles of one mealworm with petroleum jelly, another with dish detergent, a third with vegetable oil, and leave one as the control.

Look for the mealworm's first pair of legs, just behind its head. Spiracles can be found on this segment and every other segment all the way down the abdomen. There are a pair of spiracles on each side of each segment. Dip your finger in petroleum jelly and rub it along the spiracles to block them. You only need a thin layer, but be sure to cover all the spiracles on all the segments. Place this mealworm in the first foil pan. Label the pan, "petroleum jelly."

Mix 1 tablespoon of dish detergent into 1 cup of water. Pick up a mealworm and dip its abdomen and thorax into the soapy water for just a couple of seconds. Place this mealworm in the next pan and label the pan, "Soap." Now, dip another mealworm into the vegetable oil for a couple of seconds (FIG. 35-1). Place it into the next pan and label the pan, "Oil." You must apply the coatings quickly so you can observe the behavior of each at the same time, or apply the coating on the first mealworm and make all your observations before applying the coating on the next mealworm.

35-1 Study how contaminants affect insect respiration.

Place the last mealworm into the last pan and label it "Control." Do not apply any coating to this mealworm's spiracles.

Compare the movements of all four mealworms. Take notes about the amount of movement. After two or three minutes, pick each mealworm up and observe its reactions, and take notes.

After watching the insects for about one hour, pick up each mealworm and wipe off as much of the coating as possible using paper towels. Letting the mealworm move around on a paper towel will remove most of it. Return the mealworms to the pans and observe their behavior.

CONCLUSIONS

How does blocking the spiracles affect the movement of the insects? Can they survive for long with the spiracles closed? Can they recover if the spiracles are reopened? Do they each move as much? What are your conclusions?

GOING FURTHER

- Read more about insect respiration.
- Does this experiment give you any ideas about how to control insect pests?
- Consider also doing the experiment, *Behave yourself* as part of your project.

36
How high
can they go?
Jumping insects

Many insects are great jumpers. Grasshoppers, crickets, springtails, and fleas are just a few examples of jumping insects. Jumping is not only a good way to travel, but it is a quick way to escape danger. How far can insects jump? Does the size of an individual affect its jumping ability?

MATERIALS

- About 10 crickets of varying sizes (can be purchased at a pet store)
- Outdoor sandbox or similar setup
- Rake
- Ruler
- Yardstick
- Insect collecting net or aquarium net (You can use an aquarium fishnet, since you're just recapturing a single insect.)

PROCEDURES

This experiment can be done at any time of the year, as long as it is above 60 degrees Fahrenheit. Measure the body length (head to the tip of the abdomen) of a cricket. The best way to do this is to gently hold the cricket in the net while you measure it (FIG. 36-1). Don't squeeze it too hard. Write the measurement in your notes.

Now, put the cricket carefully down on the flat sand in a predesignated spot. If it doesn't move, nudge it with your finger to get it to jump. Measure the distance it jumped (it will have made a mark in the sand where it landed) and note the distance (FIG. 36-2). Recapture the insect and repeat this up to five times. You will have to smooth the sand over between jumps. Does the cricket continue to jump the same distance?

Repeat this process with at least four other individual insects, of various

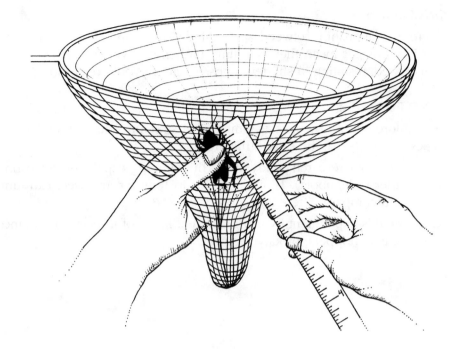

36-1 Measure the length of a cricket.

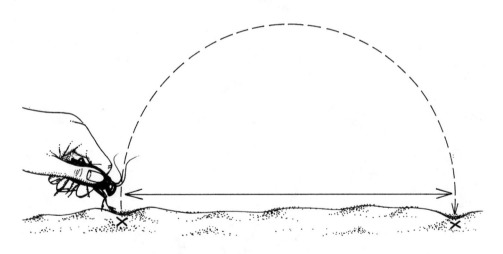

36-2 Measure the distance each different size cricket can jump.

sizes. Make notes of the distance each individual jumped, and notes on the body length of each one.

CONCLUSIONS

Is there a relationship between size of individuals and distance they can jump? Does bigger mean they can jump farther, and vice versa? Do the insects get tired, resulting in shorter jumps? What are your conclusions?

GOING FURTHER

- Read more about how insects jump. What structures do they use? Do all types of insects use the same structures?

- As part of your research, study about the jumping capabilities of springtails (order Collembola). Is size a factor in how far an insect can jump when you compare different species of insects?

- Continue this experiment by using different kinds of insects (for instance, crickets, grasshoppers, or katydids).

37
Fill'er up
Insects' digestive system

As insects eat, food enters their mouths, travels to their *foregut*, then to the *midgut* and finally to the *hindgut*. What does an insect's gut look like? How long does it take for food to enter the different parts of the gut and to fill it up? Decide on your hypothesis and proceed with the project.

MATERIALS

- Live mosquito larvae (They can be collected in warm weather from a small pool or a container filled with water and left outside for a few weeks. Or they can be purchased from a biological supply house.)
- Activated charcoal dust (aquarium charcoal is good) or other fine, colored particles (such as from dry dyes).
- A disposable container that can hold two cups (Cut-off plastic milk cartons will be perfect.)
- Eyedropper with a tip that is not too narrow
- Magnifying glass

PROCEDURES

If you plan to collect your own mosquitoes, the experiment must be done during warm weather. If you purchase mosquitoes, it can be done at any time of the year. Fill up the container with 2 cups of water. Add a few mosquito larvae to the container with the eyedropper or a spoon. Let them get used to the water for 30 minutes. Now, add the dust particles by rubbing a small amount of activated charcoal or dye between your fingers over the water. Dust will fall into the container and float on the water (FIG. 37-1). It will then gradually sink into the water.

Observe the mosquito larvae and take notes. Continue to observe the mosquito for a few minutes, every five minutes. Watch the movement of the dust as it enters and passes through the gut of the mosquito. (You can see through the skin of the mosquito.) You might want to remove the mosquito from the container every once in awhile and look at it closely with a magnifying glass (FIG. 37-2). Then return it to the container.

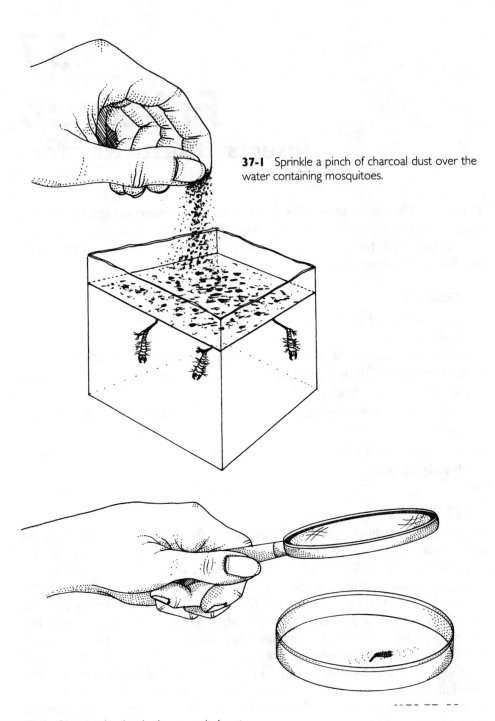

37-1 Sprinkle a pinch of charcoal dust over the water containing mosquitoes.

37-2 Observe the dust in the mosquito's gut.

Gently stir the water if the dust settles to the bottom after awhile. Take notes and draw sketches during each observation. Repeat this procedure until you have observed at least five individuals.

CONCLUSIONS

How long does it take to get the colored particles into each portion of the gut? How long does it take to get the particles all the way through the gut? Did all the individuals take about the same amount of time? Do these insects digest food rapidly or slowly?

What does the gut look like? Does it run the length of the larva's body? Where does it start and end? What does the gut consist of? What is its form, a straight tube or does it twist around like the gut of a human?

GOING FURTHER

- Read more about the structure of an insect's digestive system. Do all insects have the same type of system? Would an insect that fed on blood have the same system as one that fed on wood? Are there insects that have no digestive system at all?

- To continue this experiment, run the same experiment under different temperature conditions. Put one in the refrigerator and one under a hot lamp. Does the time it takes to fill the insects' guts change?

38
Dragons in the sky
Insects in flight

Dragonflies and damselflies (order Odonata) are often seen around ponds, lakes, and streams from late spring to early fall. They live in water during their immature stages, then crawl up and emerge into adult fliers. Their flying ability is truly amazing. They are quick and agile, capable of making 90 degree turns at high speed. Both dragonflies and damselflies are predators their entire lives: during their immature life in the water and as adults flying through the air.

Although their form is similar in many ways, dragonflies are more robust than damselflies with larger, wider bodies and wider wings. Damselflies, also called darning needles, are daintier, with a thinner body, and narrower wings (FIG. 38-1).

For what reason might dragonflies be more robust than damselflies? Is one more aggressive? Do they exhibit different types of behavior? Do both of these similar insects spend the same amount of time in the air? What is your hypothesis?

MATERIALS

- A field or meadow near a pond where you can observe dragonflies and damselflies
- Broomstick or other long stick or pole

PROCEDURES

This experiment should be done in early summer to early fall when these insects are often seen. Find an area near a pond or a lake that has both damselflies and dragonflies. Observe their behavior. Take detailed notes. Record the time they spend flying and the amount of time landed on a plant. In 30 minutes, how much time does a dragonfly spend flying compared to a damselfly? Record their flight patterns. Can you distinguish the flight pattern of dragonflies versus damselflies?

After observing them undisturbed, enter their territory near the bank of a pond and hold up a broomstick. Do they react to it? If so, how do they react? Take notes on what happens.

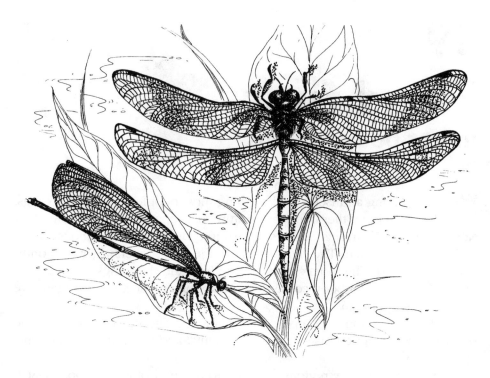

38-1 Study the differences between a dragonfly and a damselfly.

CONCLUSIONS

Analyze your data. Study the flying patterns and behavior of both. Then compare the two. What differences and what similarities can you see? What percent of the time did they each spend in the air? How did their flight patterns differ? How did they each act when you invaded their territory with the broomstick? Why might the dragonfly have a different body shape than the damselfly? What are your conclusions?

GOING FURTHER

- Read more about the biology of dragonflies and damselflies. Study their *territoriality*.
- To continue the experiment, read about dragonfly and damselfly mating behavior and then continue your observations in the field.

39
Head first
Insect body regions

When identifying an insect, the first thing most people look for is six legs. However, there is another important feature that separates insects from other closely related organisms. Insects have three distinct body regions: head, thorax, and abdomen. The head is where the eyes, antennae, and mouthparts are located. The thorax is where the legs and the wings are attached. The remainder of the body consists of the abdomen. Most of the organs are found in the abdomen.

Each body region is composed of segments. The head consists of one segment, the thorax consists of three segments, and the abdomen can have up to 12 segments.

How do these body regions compare to those of other arthropods such as a spider? Spiders have eight legs instead of an insect's six, but how does a spider's segmentation differ from insects? What is your hypothesis?

MATERIALS
- Dead cricket or other insect
- Dead spider
- Magnifying lens

PROCEDURES
You might want to use an insect and spider that you recently caught and placed in a killing jar. These specimens won't be brittle, as would an organism that had been dead a long time. This will make them easier to study under magnification (FIG. 39-1).

Find the three body regions of the cricket. Look at the insect under magnification to do this. Draw the body regions and notice the segmentation within each body region. Take notes along with the drawing. Now, look at the body of a spider. Can you find three distinct body regions? Draw whatever regions you can find. Look in your field guide for information and illustrations to help you.

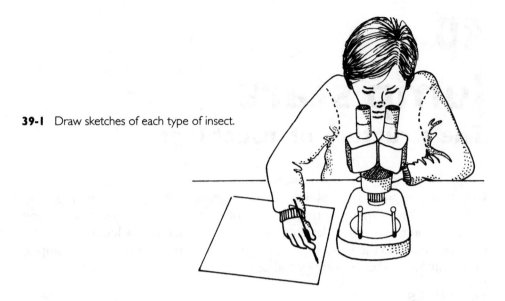

39-1 Draw sketches of each type of insect.

CONCLUSIONS

How does the spider's body regions and segmentation differ from an insect? Are these two organisms in the same class or phylum? What differences separate spiders and insects? What are your conclusions?

GOING FURTHER

- Read more about the *morphology* of adult insects. Read about how the morphology of immature insects vary.
- Continue this experiment by comparing the body regions of a tick (or a mite) to a spider and an insect. Is the tick more closely related to a spider or to an insect?

40
Jump start
The structure of insect legs

Insects get around by walking, flying, jumping, hopping, crawling, and swimming. The variety of their means of motion is astounding. Does the shape of their legs differ depending upon their method of locomotion? For example, how do the legs of a walking insect compare with that of a jumper, or a swimmer? What is your hypothesis?

MATERIALS

- A dead cricket or grasshopper (or other jumping insect)
- A dead ant or other crawling insect (Some crawling insects such as cockroaches can fly but use walking as their primary mode of locomotion, so they can be used also.)
- Dissecting microscope or magnifying glass
- Ruler (preferably a small, flat, translucent, plastic ruler)

PROCEDURE

Under magnification look at all three sets of legs on both the jumping and the walking insects (FIG. 40-1). Draw sketches of each. How are they the same? How do they differ? Identify the five parts of each leg. All three sets of legs have all five parts. It is easier to identify the leg segments by starting with the *tarsus*, which is at the tip of the leg. Use your field guide or take out an entomology book from the library to help you identify each section. Measure the thickness and length of each section for each insect and for each leg part. Fill in a table similar to TABLE 40-1.

Study your sketches and then compare the three sets of legs of each insect. Then compare the legs of the crawling insect with the jumping insect. How are they similar and how do they differ? Note your observations.

CONCLUSIONS

How are each insect's legs adapted for their type of locomotion? What role does the length of the segments and the thickness of each play? What are your conclusions? If you looked at an insect's leg, could you tell how it moves?

Table 40-1 Leg measurements

Insect type—	Thickness (mm)		
	Walking	Jumping	Swimming
Foreleg:			
Coxa			
Trochanter			
Femur			
Tibia			
Tarsus			
Midleg:			
Coxa			
Trochanter			
Femur			
Tibia			
Tarsus			
Hindleg:			
Coxa			
Trochanter			
Femur			
Tibia			
Tarsus			

Table 40-1 Continued

Insect type—	Length (mm)		
	Walking	Jumping	Swimming
Foreleg:			
Coxa			
Trochanter			
Femur			
Tibia			
Tarsus			
Midleg:			
Coxa			
Trochanter			
Femur			
Tibia			
Tarsus			
Hindleg:			
Coxa			
Trochanter			
Femur			
Tibia			
Tarsus			

40-1 Aquatic insects have legs with unique adaptations for their environment.

GOING FURTHER

- Read more about how insects have adapted for various types of locomotion.

- To continue this experiment, collect from a pond or stream (or purchase from a biological supply house) an aquatic insect such as a water strider or water boatman. Compare the leg parts of these swimming insects to the legs of a crawling or jumping insect. How do they differ? (Be careful, aquatic insects can bite!)

41
All dried up
The insect's exoskeleton and water loss

As you know, insects are small creatures. Small animals have a high *surface area* to *volume ratio*. Surface area means the amount of the organism that is exposed to the environment. Volume means the overall size of the organism. The ratio is a method of comparing the two. The surface area to volume ratio is important because it is one of the factors that determines how quickly water evaporates from the organism's body. A normal-sized ant would lose a higher percentage of its water than an ant the size of an elephant, because an elephant-sized ant has a much lower surface area to volume ratio.

Since small animals have a high surface area to volume ratio, they must try to prevent water loss as much as possible, or they will dry up and die. An insect's exoskeleton is covered by a *cuticle* (skin) consisting of fats and waxes. Does wax reduce water evaporation? Do these substances keep the insect from drying up? Form your hypothesis and proceed with the experiment. This project involves no live insects.

MATERIALS
- Two bottles of the same size with openings approximately 2 inches in diameter (16 ounce juice bottles would work well)
- Two bottles of the same size with openings approximately ½ inch in diameter (16 ounce vinegar bottles would work well)
- Candle
- Matches
- Rubber cement
- Pin
- Ruler

PROCEDURES
This experiment can be done at any time of the year. The first two bottles will represent an insect's surface without any wax cover. Cut out two pieces

of paper: One that fits the dimensions of the 2-inch bottle opening and the other to fit the smaller bottle opening. Fill the two bottles with water, all the way to the top of the rim. Next, put a thin layer of rubber cement around the top edge of the mouth lip on both bottles. Glue the paper pieces to the tops of these bottles and set them aside.

The next two bottles will represent an insect's cuticle containing a wax layer. Fill the other two bottles to the rim with water. Light the candle. Hold the candle over the bottles, so the wax drips onto the water's surface. Continue dripping wax until the surface is completely covered (FIG. 41-1). The wax should drip over the outside edges of the bottles, to make a tight seal. Let the wax harden.

41-1 Drip the wax over the water's surface at the rim of the bottle.

Since insects have holes throughout their surface for breathing, called spiracles, take the straight pin and gently punch two small holes through the center of all four bottle coverings, paper and wax.

Set aside the bottles for six weeks. Keep all the bottles in the same environment. Most importantly, be sure they are equally exposed to the same temperature.

After six weeks, mark the level of water in each bottle. Are the water levels equal or did one lose more water than another?

CONCLUSIONS

Did the wax reduce evaporation more than the paper? Did the surface area (the size of the openings) have an effect on the evaporation rate? Relate what you have learned to an insect's surface area to volume ratio. What are your conclusions?

GOING FURTHER

- Read more about water loss in insects (called *desiccation*).
- Perform the same experiment but make twice as many bottles, and leave one set in direct sunlight and the other out of the light. How are the results different and why?

Part 5

Insects and Humans

Insects are involved in almost every aspect of our lives and have been throughout history. The life of man and the life of insects are closely intertwined. Insects provide us with products that we use, such as honey and silk. They perform services that we could not live without, such as pollinating plants, and they can cause enormous destruction by spreading disease and eating our crops. The relationships between insects and humans are fascinating to study.

The projects in this section study insects that are either helpful or harmful to us, and one project studies how helpful insects are used to control harmful ones.

42
Repelling creatures
Insect repellents and attractants

Insects are pests to more than our food supply. They can be particularly annoying when WE are their food supply! There are many blood-sucking insects: mosquitoes, black flies, green heads, deer flies, horse flies and no-see-ums, just to name a few. Blood-feeding insects bother more than just humans; they're a pest of other mammals, birds, reptiles, and even frogs.

Blood feeders find their meal by sensing carbon dioxide that is exhaled with each breath we take. We can't stop breathing to get relief, but we can use an insect repellent. Does an insect repellent stop the insect from being attracted to the carbon dioxide or simply prevent the insect from landing on the host? State your hypothesis and then proceed with the experiment.

MATERIALS
- Two plastic-coated paper plates (about 8 inches in diameter)
- Talcum powder
- Mineral oil
- Small bowl to mix powder and oil
- Small paintbrush or basting brush to spread the mixture
- Two bookends (or anything that will prop up the paper plates)
- Four large paper clips (1.5 inches)
- An outdoor table
- Dry ice, 2 to 3 lbs. (CAUTION: always use tongs and gloves when handling dry ice. Do not touch it with your bare hands, and have adult supervision at all times.)
- Plastic bowl to hold the dry ice
- Spray-on insect repellent (use a repellent that has DEET as the active ingredient)

PROCEDURES

Late spring until early fall is usually the best time for this project. Label one plate "with repellent" and the other "without repellent." Attach one plate to a bookend with two paper clips. If you don't have a bookend, use anything that will hold the plate up in a vertical position. Repeat with the other plate and another bookend (FIG. 42-1).

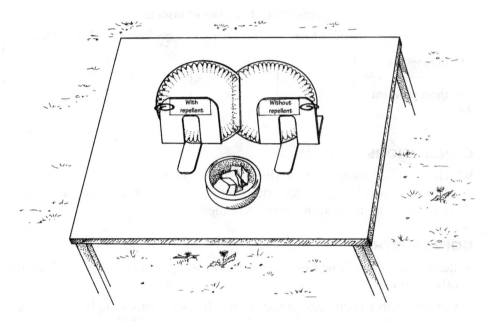

42-1 This is the setup to test how insect repellents work.

Now, mix 1 part mineral oil with 3 to 4 parts talcum powder in the bowl. Use enough talc to create a stiff paste. Spread the mixture over both plates with the brush. Cover the same area on each plate. This mixture will trap any insects that come in contact with the plates. Gently spray the plate labeled "repellent" with the insect repellent.

Place a table outside. For best results, choose an area where you have seen or been bitten by biting insects such as mosquitoes. Put the sticky plates on the table, side-by-side. Place the dry ice (Do not use your hands—use tongs) in a bowl in front of and evenly between the two propped-up sticky plates as you see in the illustration. Position the dry ice so as it melts, both sticky plates are exposed to equal amounts of gaseous carbon dioxide.

Mid- to late afternoon is the best time to start this experiment, and it should be a windless day. A windy day might blow the plates away and will cause an uneven distribution of the carbon dioxide flow over the plates. If there is a mild wind, position the plates and bowl so the wind is blowing toward the plates.

Check the plates every few hours and around dusk. Leave the plates in place overnight and check them again the next morning. During each observation, count the number of insects stuck to each plate and write down the results in a table similar to TABLE 42-1.

Table 42-1   Number of insects

	One hour	Four hours	Eight hours	Twenty-four hours
With repellent				
Without repellent				

CONCLUSIONS

Which plate had more insects? Did the repellent appear to work? Since insects flying around both plates could sense the carbon dioxide, what conclusions can you make about your hypothesis?

GOING FURTHER

- Read more about how insects find a host to feed upon. Do they use any other senses?

- Continue this experiment to see what other substances might work as an insect repellent. Test them as you have just done with the commercial repellent. Are there substances that you think might act as an insect attractant, such as perfumes? Test them also.

- You can continue this experiment to see if there is a certain time of day when biting flies are most common. Run this test without repellent at different times. Do you get different numbers of insects at different times? Do you get different kinds of insects at different times?

43

Silky smooth
Silk and sericulture

Silk is the finest of all natural fibers. It is strong, smooth, and light in weight, yet has great insulation properties. *Sericulture* is the name of the silk production industry. The insect used in sericulture is the silkworm. Its scientific name is *Bombyx mori*. There are, however, many insects and other arthropods such as spiders and mites that can produce silk. Butterflies and moths (in the order Lepidoptera) all use silk in their cocoons.

Does the silk of the silkworm differ from the silk of other insects and arthropods? Is one stronger than the other? How does this silk differ from commercial silk thread that you can purchase? State your hypotheses and then proceed with the project.

MATERIALS

- Silkworm cocoon (available from biological supply houses)
- A cocoon of any moth or butterfly (collected from outside or ordered from a biological supply house)
- Spider web (that you've found)
- Dissecting microscope or a good-quality magnifying glass
- Commercial, 100-percent silk thread (from a fabric store)
- Straight pin
- Bowl, about pint-sized
- Piece of cardboard, approx. 4 inches square
- Black marking pen

PROCEDURES

This experiment can be performed at any time of year. You will create a silk sample board as you see in the illustration (FIG. 43-1), which will be studied beneath a dissecting microscope or a magnifying glass.

Color a 3-inch-square area on the cardboard black with the marking pen. The black background will help you see the silk. Prepare each cocoon by soaking them for thirty minutes in warm water. This loosens the silk strands

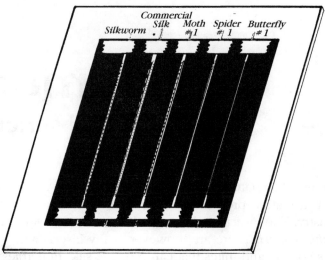

43-1 Use a silk sample board to study how silk produced by various organisms differs.

from the gummy material that surrounds them, making it easier to get the silk threads out of the cocoons.

Look at each of the cocoons under the microscope or magnifying glass. Use the straight pin and tease loose an individual silk thread from each cocoon surface.

Moth cocoons will probably have a hardened outside silk mass, that encloses the finer silk cocoon inside. Cut away this outside silk layer with scissors and peel it back to expose the fine layers inside.

Unwind a thread of silk from each cocoon about 3 inches long. Cut it off the cocoon with scissors. Tape each end of the silk thread to the cardboard, leaving a 2-inch length of thread untaped in the middle (FIG. 43-1).

Now cut out a 3-inch length from a spider web. Some of the silk in the spider web may look different from other threads in the same web (especially if you're using an orb web, rather than a cobweb). Attach examples of spider web silk on the cardboard in the same manner as explained above.

Finally, cut a thread of the commercial, 100-percent silk thread you purchased and tape it to the board in the same manner. Label each type of thread on the cardboard with the pencil as you tape them to the board.

Use the microscope or magnifying glass to look at the threads on the cardboard. Which ones are thicker? Are some of these threads actually made up of multiple strands? Gently rub each strand back and forth with the side of the pin to separate strands that may be entwined together. How many individual strands are present in each type of silk? Compare the color of each. Do they differ in appearance or size? Fill in a table with your data (TABLE 43-1).

Table 43-1   Silk characteristics

Thread	Color	Relative thickness	Number of strands / thread	Comments e.g., texture, stretchability
Silkworm				
Com. silk				
Moth #1				
Spider #1				
Butterfly #1				

CONCLUSIONS

Analyze the data. Are all forms of silk the same or do they differ? If there are differences, how do they differ and why do you think they differ? What are your conclusions?

GOING FURTHER

- Read more about sericulture and the silkworm.
- Read about how spider webs are created and how they work.
- Continue this experiment by studying how strong a single strand of silk is. Tie small fishing weights to each type of silk. How much can they support before they break?

44
The teeny tiny wasp
Biocontrol of insect pests

Insects can be extremely destructive to our crops. Much of our food is also food for insects. Farmers must continually battle insect populations to raise their crops. They use a number of weapons in this fight, including chemical insecticides and physical barriers. *Biocontrol* (also called biological control) is a newer method of fighting insect pests without using harmful chemicals.

Many insects eat other insects. Insects that eat and destroy harmful insects can be used to help us control these pests. Using beneficial insects to control harmful insects is called biocontrol or biological control. The beneficial insects are called biocontrol agents. There are three kinds of biocontrol agents being used to control insect pests.

Predators usually attack, kill, and eat other individuals. Predators eat many other organisms, called *prey,* as they grow to maturity. *Parasites* live on another organism and feed on it, but don't usually kill the organism, called a *host.* Parasites may live on more than one host during its lifetime. *Parasitoids* feed on only one host their entire life and usually end up killing the host.

There are many tiny parasitoid wasps. These parasitoid wasps are harmless to humans. One wasp that is frequently used for biocontrol in greenhouses is called *Trichogramma minutens.* (That's its scientific name. It doesn't have a common name.) This wasp is an egg parasitoid, since the adult female wasp lays its eggs in another insect's egg. The immature wasp hatches out of its egg (within the host egg) and eats the inside of the host egg for nourishment. When it is fully grown, it emerges out of the host egg as an adult wasp.

This wasp is sometimes used as a biocontrol agent, since it often lays its eggs in a common garden pest, the tobacco hornworm. How long does it take for the wasp to emerge as an adult from within the egg? How many wasps can live and emerge from one parasitized egg? State your hypothesis and proceed with the experiment.

Although these wasps are visible to the naked eye, they are very small and will require most of the work to be done under a dissecting microscope or a high-quality magnifying lens.

MATERIALS

- 10 Tobacco Hornworm eggs, parasitized by *Trichogramma minutens* (from a biological supply house or an organic gardening nursery)
- 10 deep saucers (about ½ inch high and 4 inches in diameter) that can be tightly closed, or petri dishes
- Fine forceps
- Small paintbrush (model plane paintbrush)
- Honey
- Spoon
- Dissecting microscope or high-quality magnifying glass

PROCEDURES

This experiment can be done at any time in the year. Put a single parasitized egg in each of the 10 dishes. Be careful separating the egg from the egg mass. Use either fine forceps or a fine brush (FIG. 44-1) Parasitized eggs are dark colored. Don't use green eggs, since they aren't parasitized.

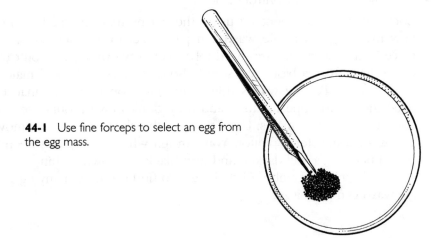

44-1 Use fine forceps to select an egg from the egg mass.

Place a tiny drop of honey in each dish. Now close the dish and seal it with tape so the wasps cannot escape. If they do escape, they won't hurt anything, but your experiment will be ruined. Keep the dishes at room temperature.

Each day, check each dish for adult wasps. They are small, so look at the dish with the magnifying glass or microscope. Look around the honey drop, since the first thing they will do after emerging is eat. Continue to observe them every day for four weeks. When they emerge, count the number of wasps in each dish. Note your observations for each dish.

CONCLUSIONS

How long did it take before the adult emerged? How many wasps can come out of each egg? Create a chart (TABLE 44-1), and fill in your data. Analyze the data. What are your conclusions about your original hypothesis? Do you think these wasps could be used successfully as a biocontrol agent?

Table 44-1   Dish number

	1	2	3	4	5	6	7	8	9	10
Number of wasps to emerge from egg										

GOING FURTHER

- Read more about biocontrol of pests.
- Continue the experiment by using the wasps that emerged to find out how many eggs a single wasp can parasitize. In another set of dishes, place 5, 10, and 50 unparasitized tobacco hornworm eggs. (You can purchase them from a biological supply house.) Place a single female wasp in each dish. Female wasps don't have hairs on their antennae (you'll need the microscope for this) and they don't move around very much compared with the males. Use a tiny paintbrush to pick up and move the wasps, or a transfer aspirator. You can tell when an egg has been parasitized because it will darken and turn black or brown within one to two weeks. Count the number of dark eggs to find out how many eggs a single wasp can parasitize.

45

As sweet
as can bee

Honeybee feeding

Honeybees are responsible for a substantial part of our food supply. Humans depend on honeybees to pollinate fruit trees, small berries, and many forage plants that our domesticated animals eat. These plants cannot produce seeds or fruits without first being pollinated by a bee. Plants get insects to pollinate them by producing a sugar solution, called *nectar,* that the insects use for food.

Bees fly from flower to flower to collect the nectar. As they do this, they pick up pollen from one flower and deliver it to another flower of the same species. This results in seed production and plant reproduction.

Nectar is the reward the plant provides for the bee's pollination services. The plant, however, must use its own food to produce nectar. Sugar that goes into nectar is less food for the plant itself, so a high sugar concentration in the nectar is costly to the plant. It would be worthwhile for the plant to produce nectar with as little sugar in it as possible, yet still attract the bees.

Can bees detect low sugar concentrations? Do bees respond to increased sugar concentrations? Is there a sugar concentration level that wastes sugar? What are your hypotheses?

WARNING: This experiment involves observing bees. Follow the instructions carefully and always have adult supervision. If you are allergic to bee stings, do not attempt this experiment.

MATERIALS

- Six saucers about 4 inches in diameter, that can hold about ½ inch of fluid (or the bottom of a petri dish)
- Six containers for mixing sugar solutions (They should hold about 2 cups of liquid.)
- Granulated sugar

- Teaspoon and tablespoon
- Measuring cup

PROCEDURES

Choose a sunny, warm day for the best results. Early spring to late summer is the best time of the year for this experiment but you'll find bees flying on warm, sunny winter days.

You will make 5 sugar solutions, mixing 2 cups of water with the following amounts of sugar.

- *concentration #1* = 1½ teaspoons
- *concentration #2* = 3 teaspoons
- *concentration #3* = 6 teaspoons
- *concentration #4* = ¼ cup + 3 teaspoons
- *concentration #5* = ½ cup + 6 teaspoons

For the first concentration, put 2 cups of water in a container labeled "#1." Add 1½ teaspoons of granulated sugar. Stir the solution so the sugar is completely dissolved. Label a dish "#1" and pour in 2 tablespoons of the "#1" solution.

Repeat these steps for concentrations two through five. Clean off the spoon between each use. Label the sixth dish "plain water" and pour in 2 tablespoons of water.

Arrange the dishes on a box or a table outside in an area where you have seen honeybees flying about. They can be placed outside, prior to sunrise, before the bees are out of their nests. Leave the area to observe the bees from a distance (FIG. 45-1). You can even use binoculars or set the table up outside a window, so observations can be made from indoors.

Observe the bees for one hour once they have become active. Write down the starting time of the experiment, what time each dish was first visited by bees, and the approximate number of bees visiting each dish in ten minute intervals (TABLE 45-1). Also, watch to see if some dishes run out of liquid before other dishes. Write down the time a dish empties.

WARNING: Be very careful when removing or refilling the dishes. Bees may be on or in the dish. You might want to wait until the sun sets, when the bees are back in their nests. Use gloves when picking up the dishes, just in case.

CONCLUSIONS

From your notes, answer the following questions. Do the bees visit all the dishes equally? If not, which are visited the most and which the least? Analyze your data. A graph might help you understand the results. From this

45-1 Observe which sugar solutions honeybees prefer.

Table 45-1 Time in minutes

Concentration	10	20	30	40	50	60
1						
2						
3						
4						
5						
6						

information, can you conclude that bees can sense the different concentrations of sugar? Is there a minimum sugar concentration that they can sense? Is there a maximum concentration? How might a maximum concentration be important to the plant? What are your conclusions?

GOING FURTHER

- Read more about honeybee feeding behavior.
- Investigate whether there are other kinds of insects that feed on nectar and pollinate plants besides bees.
- Consider also doing the project *How sweet is it?* as part of your science fair project.
- To continue with this experiment, place a piece of blue paper under the dish that was visited the most by bees. Refill the dish with the sugar water at the same time of day for a few days. Then, move the blue paper and put it under the plain water dish. What dish do the bees first visit: the blue dish or the dish with sugar?

46
How sweet is it?
Insects and food

In some parts of the world, insects are eaten by humans: roasted giant water bugs are snacks in Southeast Asia, baked locusts in northern Africa, and gnats in central Africa. Americans don't generally eat insects, but we do consume a product made by insects, honey.

Honeybees fly from flower to flower, collecting nectar from the plant. They store this nectar in a part of their digestive system called the *crop.* When their crop is full, they return to their hive and regurgitate the nectar into a cell in the honeycomb. Other bees do the same until the cell is full.

Over time, the water in this solution evaporates, and what remains is honey. Honey is simply the evaporated nectar from plants, collected and tended by honeybees. The honey is meant to be used by the bees as food for their young, but we often have other plans for the honey. People use honey in place of sugar while baking and cooking, and to sweeten cereal, tea, or coffee.

How much sugar is in honey? How does an equal volume of honey compare in sugar content with the same volume of sugar purchased from a store? What is your hypothesis? This project involves no live insects.

MATERIALS
- Honey
- Fructose or glucose sugar (You can purchase these at a grocery store. Don't use regular cane sugar!)
- ⅛, ¼, ½, and 1 teaspoon measures
- Marker that writes on glass
- Eyedropper
- Quantitative Benedict solution (available from a biological supply house or possibly your school laboratory)
- Small pot, approximately 1 pint pan
- Test tube holder or an oven mitt
- Five similar test tubes (about 6 inches long and ⅜ inch in diameter)
- Ruler

PROCEDURES

This experiment can be done at any time in the year. You will create a series of sugar solutions and test the sugar contents of each with Benedict solution. Use the ruler to measure ½ inch up from the bottom of each test tube. Draw a line on the glass at this level for each tube. Measure ½ teaspoon of sugar (fructose or glucose, not sucrose) and pour it into one of the test tubes. Label this tube "½ tsp." Using the eyedropper, add in enough water to bring the level to the ½ inch line on the tube. Swirl the tube until the sugar is dissolved.

In another tube, measure in ¼ teaspoon of sugar, and label this tube "¼ tsp." Again, add enough water to bring the level to the ½-inch line on the tube and swirl until dissolved. In a third tube, add in ⅛ teaspoon of sugar. Label this tube "⅛ tsp." Add water up to the line and swirl the tube.

In a fourth tube, add water up to the line and label this tube "blank." Finally, in a fifth tube, add ½ teaspoon of honey. Label this tube "honey." Add water to bring the fluid level up to the ½-inch line. Swirl to dissolve the honey. You might have to stir the contents to get them to dissolve.

Once all the tubes are mixed and labeled, add 2.5 teaspoons of Benedict solution to each tube.

Now boil water in a small pot. The water should only be about 2 inches high in the pan. Place the test tubes in the boiling water for two to three minutes as illustrated (FIG. 46-1). The tops of the test tubes must be well above the water's surface. When you are finished heating the tubes, use an oven mitt or a test tube holder to remove them from the pot.

What are the colors of the solutions in each test tube? Fill in a table

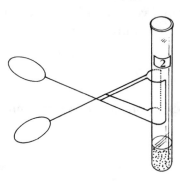
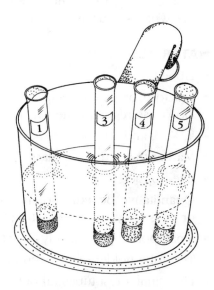

46-1 Heat up all the test tubes containing the Benedict solution.

(TABLE 46-1) with your data. Benedict solution turns yellow to a brownish-yellow, depending on how much sugar is present: the more sugar the darker the color. After the tubes cool, look for a *precipitate* (a solid material that sinks to the bottom of the tube). Do all the tubes have a precipitate? More precipitate means more sugar was present. Do they all have the same amount of precipitate?

Table 46-1

Test tube number	Color	Precipitate yes/no	Relative amount of precipitate
1			
2			
3			
4			
5			

CONCLUSIONS

Analyze your data. What conclusions can you draw about the amount of sugar in honey compared with sugar? Can you tell how much sugar there is in 1 teaspoon of honey from this experiment?

GOING FURTHER

- Read more about honey production and the feeding behavior of honeybees.

- Consider doing *Sweet as can bee* as part of your project.

- Continue this experiment by determining how much sugar there is in honey. How much sugar must be added to get the same reaction as with the same volume of honey? Keep increasing the amount of sugar until it turns the same color and has as much precipitate as the honey. How much is necessary?

47
Unwelcome guests
Survey of insects inhabiting buildings

Insects have shared our buildings ever since we started making them. What kinds of insects usually live with us in buildings? In this project you will create an insect *survey collection*.

A survey collection contains all the insects found in a certain area or habitat. In this case, the habitat is buildings. Once a survey collection is made, it can be studied to draw conclusions about the insect population in that habitat. How many kinds of insects, representing how many orders, can be found within buildings? Are there a few or many insect orders represented in a collection of these unwelcome guests? State your hypothesis.

MATERIALS
- 10 wide-mouthed jars (32-ounce mayonnaise jars, or quart-size canning jars)
- Petroleum jelly
- Coffee filters (No. 4 size, cone-shaped)
- Newspaper
- Masking tape
- Oats
- Banana slices
- Honey
- Five yeast cakes
- Nail polish remover
- Cotton balls
- Small plastic bags to hold insects collected in the jars
- Plastic bags (to fit over mouth of jar)
- Rubber bands (to go around mouth of jar)

PROCEDURES

This experiment can be done at any time in the year. You will make 10 insect traps which will be placed in various locations in buildings. The traps allow insects to crawl into the jar, but not escape.

To make a trap, put a layer of petroleum jelly on the upper inside edge of the jar, about ½ inch from the top. The petroleum jelly should be approximately ⅛ inch thick and ¼ inch wide. This keeps insects from crawling back out of the bottle.

Cut a 1-inch hole in the tip of a coffee filter. Put the filter two thirds of the way into the mouth of the bottle and fold the upper edge of the filter over the outside edge of the jar, as you see in the illustration (FIG. 47-1). This helps the insects get in but makes it difficult to get out.

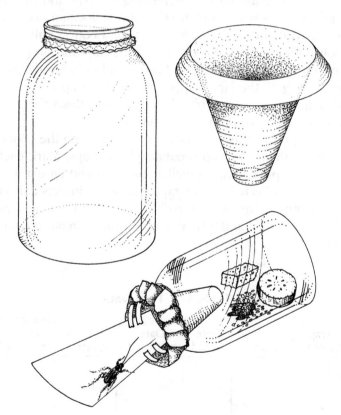

47-1 Create a baited insect trap.

Now you'll make a ramp, so it's easy for crawling insects to enter the jar. Cut a 2-by-4-inch piece of newspaper. Tape it to the edge of the cone, to make a ramp as you see in the illustration. You now have a complete, unbaited trap.

Just before use, remove the paper cone and ramp so you can bait the trap. Place a slice of banana, a spoonful of oats, a drop of honey, and half of a moistened yeast cake in each jar. Replace the cone with the ramp, and you now have a baited trap. Repeat this process for all 10 traps.

These traps should be placed in homes and other buildings where insects might be found. Basements, kitchens, bathrooms, storage areas, and garages are all good trap sites. The traps should be placed against a wall, in out-of-the-way spots. Dark, damp places are usually good for catching insects. Write down the date and time you set the traps and the location of each, so you can find them in a few days. The traps should be left in place for three to seven days.

When enough time has passed, return to each location. If a trap has no insects, you can reuse the trap by refreshing the bait and making sure the petroleum jelly layer is still complete. Find a new location for that particular trap. For the traps that do contain insects, take a cotton ball and dampen it with nail polish remover. Take the cone off the trap and drop in the cotton. Cover the trap with the plastic bag and use a rubber band to hold it in place. Continue collecting all the jars in this manner. If a trap is found in disarray and the bait is gone, mice are probably the culprits. Reset the trap at another location since the mice will most likely return.

After the trapped insects have been in the jars with the cotton for about two hours, dump them out into separate plastic bags. Mark each bag with the building and trap location, as well as the date and time it was collected.

After you have collected all the traps, count the insects collected at each trap. Try to identify as many as possible with an insect field guide. Keep track of what was found and where it was found. Create a table and fill in your data (TABLE 47-1).

Table 47-1 Trap Data

Trap number	Location	Date placed	Date retrieved	Types of insects	Number of insects collected
1					
2					
3					
4					
5					

CONCLUSIONS

What kinds of insects did you collect? Where did you collect the most insects? Did you get different kinds of insects at different sites? How many different insect orders were found? Do many different kinds of insects inhabit buildings or only a few? Was your hypothesis correct?

GOING FURTHER

- Read more about insects that invade our homes and buildings. How do we try to control these pests?
- To continue this experiment, use different baits: apples, vegetables, dog food, etc. Do you catch different insects or do they remain the same?

48

Don't track that all over my house!

Insects and disease

Insects spread disease in many ways. They can bite and inject disease-causing (pathogenic) microorganisms such as malaria and yellow fever. Another way they spread disease is by physically moving pathogens over the foods we eat, which is called *mechanical transmission.* In this experiment, you'll track the path of a flying insect and a crawling insect within an enclosed box to see the potential for disease transmission.

Do both flying and crawling insects pose a threat in carrying and transporting pathogenic organisms? State your hypothesis and proceed with the project.

MATERIALS

- One adult housefly (these can be caught or purchased)
- One cockroach or cricket. (Cockroaches and crickets can be caught. Crickets can be purchased in pet stores.)
- Two cardboard boxes, the same size (approximately 15.5 inches long × 10.5 inches high × 12.25 inches wide, with lids and hand holes in their sides).
- Flat black spray paint
- Petri dish (approximately ½-inch high × 4-inch diameter) or saucer of similar dimensions
- Talcum powder
- Granulated sugar
- Banana
- Tablespoon measure
- Duct tape
- Pointed knife

- An aspirator (for capturing the flying insect and transferring it into the box)

PROCEDURES

This experiment can be done at any time in the year. You will create two sealed boxes, painted black on the inside, to track the path of the insect in the box.

Cover the hand holes of the boxes with duct tape. Place the tape over any folds, tears, or openings on the inside of the boxes so an insect cannot escape. Spray paint the inside of the boxes and tops black. Allow the boxes to completely dry.

Put 2 tablespoons of sugar on the dish and add a 2-inch banana slice to each dish. This will be the insect's food source and our hypothetical source of pathogens to be dispersed by our insects. Now, shake a thin layer of talcum powder over most (but not all) of the sugar and bananas on each dish. This will cover the insects as they feed and help us track their path around the box. Place these dishes on the box lids, which are sitting upside down.

Place the first box upside down on the lid. Cut a small cross in the duct tape that covers the box handles. This will let you insert the end of the aspirator (FIG. 48-1). Use the aspirator to put the flying insect into this box. Place the crawling insect into the second box and immediately place the box over the lid.

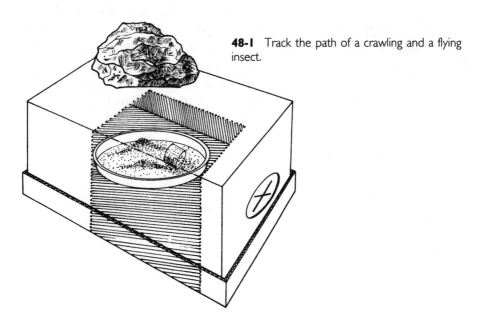

48-1 Track the path of a crawling and a flying insect.

Weigh both boxes down so the insects cannot escape under the edges. Use more duct tape, if necessary, over the edges if the lid doesn't make a tight fit with the box. Don't shake or move the box, though.

The next day, carefully take the box outside and slowly lift the box off the lid. Try not to disturb the dish containing the food and the talcum powder. Turn the boxes over and look inside. Remove the insects, or just let them fly or crawl away. Observe the talcum powder tracks made by either insect. Take notes on the tracks left in the box and draw sketches illustrating these tracks.

How many tracks are there? Where in the box are they found? Can you distinguish between the crawling and flying insect tracks? Be sure to look on all four walls for tiny track markings of either insect feet or wings.

CONCLUSIONS

Which of these insects would carry and transmit more pathogenic microorganisms that might have been in or on the food? Which types of pathogenic transmission would each type of insect most likely cause, biting or mechanical? If you did not get sufficient results, you can use the same box over again, but try different types of insects.

GOING FURTHER

- Read more about disease transmission by insects. Medical entomology is a fascinating field to study. Study how man has successfully and unsuccessfully tried to prevent diseases spread by insects.

- Continue this experiment by researching how insects transport disease through their droppings. Try the same experiment without talcum powder and with a box painted white on the inside. How many insect droppings will one individual produce over one or two days? If these droppings contained pathogens, would this be a form of disease transmission?

49
Home sweet home
Insects in the home

There are many insects that live in close association with man. Some are parasites on the human body, such as head lice and bed bugs. Some insects find our homes perfect places to live and eat. These insects include silverfish, booklice, termites, and flour beetles. The most well-known resident, however, is the cockroach. Cockroaches are found almost everywhere man is found. They can be difficult pests to get rid of, since they can eat any number of things and make their home out of almost anything.

What is a cockroach's favorite habitat? What kinds of materials do they like and dislike? In this project, you'll test different bedding materials to see which the cockroaches like and dislike. Read below about the bedding materials used in the experiment and state your hypothesis.

MATERIALS
- Five cockroaches (These can be collected by putting out traps baited with sweets in an area with a roach infestation, or be purchased from a biological supply house.)
- Two shoe boxes
- Nylon material
- Plastic packing tape
- Cardboard
- Newspapers
- Plastic sheet (such as a plastic grocery bag or garbage bag)
- Sand
- Four pieces of dry dog food

PROCEDURES
You will make a four-section cage with the shoe boxes as seen in the illustration (FIG. 49-1). Cut each box in half (width-wise). Tape all four halves together in a cross shape as you see in the illustration. On the inside of the

boxes, tape any crevices and holes shut. Tape a piece of cardboard to act as a floor for the middle section of the cross, since it will be missing a floor. Tape up all the edges so an insect can't escape.

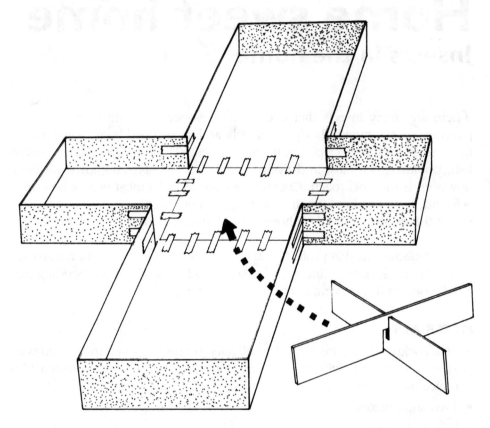

49-1 This is the initial setup to test the preferred bedding material of cockroaches.

Now you'll fill each portion of the box with a different bedding material for the cockroaches. Cut some newspaper strips and place them in one of the four portions of the box. They should be loosely packed. Fill another portion with 1 inch of dry sand. Fill the next portion with damp newspapers (not dripping wet), placed on top of a plastic sheet to keep the box from getting wet. Leave the fourth and last portion of the box empty. It will just have the cardboard floor of the shoe box.

Now you'll supply food for the creatures. Slightly moisten the dog food by putting five drops of water on each of four pieces. Place one piece in each of the four portions of the box, as far from the center of the box as possible.

Cover the top of each of the four portions of the box with nylon material. Tape the material to the boxes to hold it on. Do not cover the center of the box yet, but have a piece of nylon cut and ready. This must be left open until the insects have been placed inside.

Drop the cockroaches out of their trap into the center of the box. Quickly cover the center of the box with the nylon and tape it shut. Be sure you have taped all the holes. Leave the cage undisturbed for one week in a darkened room (or cover with newspapers so the roaches think it's dark).

Before the week has past, you must prepare for the next step of the experiment by making a barrier that keeps the insects from leaving one portion of the box and entering another. This will let you see where they have been living for the past week. To create this barrier, cut two pieces of cardboard to fit kitty-corner into the center of the box. Put a center cut halfway up the middle of each piece so they can be fitted together to form an **X**.

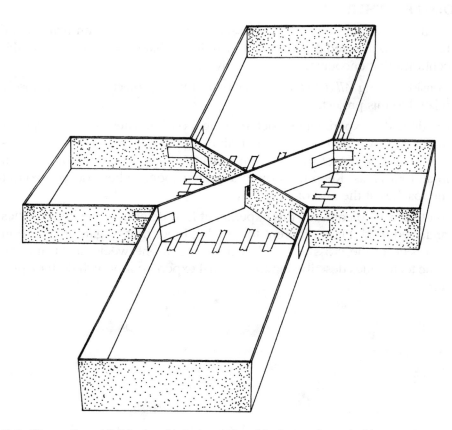

49-2 The cardboard "X" is placed into the center of the box at the end of the experiment.

At the end of the week, take the box arrangement outside (in case any insects get loose). Carefully remove the center nylon piece and quickly put the cardboard X in place so the insects are trapped in the portions of the box where they have been residing (FIG. 49-2). Tape the cross in place. Tape the nylon back on the top of the cross so the roaches cannot crawl out.

Now count all the insects in each section of the box. You might need to remove the nylon cover for each section as you examine it. Note how many insects were found in each section.

CONCLUSIONS

Does one portion have more insects than any other? Which did they like the most and which the least? Can you conclude that cockroaches prefer a particular bedding material as a habitat over any other? Why do you think one is preferable to another?

GOING FURTHER

- Read more about domesticated insects (insects that live with man). How have insects affected the history of mankind? What have we done over the centuries that encourages insects to live with us?

- Consider doing *All dried up* also as part of your project, since it is closely related to this project.

- Continue this experiment by determining if cockroaches prefer the light or the dark. Cover two of the four sections of the box with black construction paper, on top of the nylon material. Use the same bedding material in all four areas. Keep the box in a lighted room. Where do you collect the roaches at the end of a week?

- Another way to continue this experiment is to determine the cockroaches preferred food. Place different foods (dog food, fruit, sugar, or cereal) in each side of the cross and collect the roaches one week later using the same techniques described in the original experiment. Which do they prefer?

Biological supply houses

The Carolina Biological Supply Company
2700 York Road
Burlington, NC 27215
In the eastern half of the country: 800-334-5551
In the western half of the country: 800-547-1733

Live and preserved insects, insect collecting gear, and scientific supplies.

Ward's Natural Science Establishment, Inc.
5100 West Henrietta Road
Rochester, NY 14692
800-962-2660

Live and preserved insects, insect collecting gear, and scientific supplies.

Fisher Scientific
4901 W. LeMoyne Street
Chicago, IL 60651
800-955-1177

Edmund Scientific Company
101 E. Gloucester Pike
Barrington, NJ 08007
609-573-6250

Sargent-Welch Scientific Company
7300 North Linder Avenue
Skokie, IL 60077
312-677-0600

Glossary

abdomen One of the three major body divisions of an insect, containing most of the internal organs.

biocontrol The use of organisms to control pest populations, also called biological control.

cephalothorax Two of the three major body regions (head and thorax) combined into one, as in Arachnids (spiders).

collecting aspirator A device for collecting insects that uses suction.

control A part of an experiment used as a baseline.

coxa The first segment of an insect leg.

diapause A period of little or no activity.

dessication The loss of all water.

exoskeleton The external supporting and protective structure of an insect.

femur The third segment of an insect leg.

gall An insect-induced growth on a plant used for protection by the insect.

habituation The gradual reduction of a response to an event such as a stimulus.

leaf miner An insect that spends part of its life living within a leaf. It burrows tunnels (mines) as it feeds which also provide protection.

leaf roller An insect that curls part of a leaf around its body for protection during an immature stage.

mechanical control A method of controlling insect pests in which control is achieved by a mechanical means, such as using oil to block the insects' spiracles.

metamorphosis The change in body form during an insect's development.

ovipositor The external female reproductive organ used to lay eggs.

paedogenesis The ability of an immature stage of an organism to produce young.

parasite An organism that lives in or on one or more organisms (host) for a portion of its life. The host is not killed in the process.

parasitoid An insect that lives in another organism (host) and kills its host during its development.

parthenogenetic reproduction The ability to reproduce without a mate, reproduction without the fertilization of the egg.

pathogens Organisms that cause disease in other organisms.

population dynamics The study of populations and factors that affect them.

pheromone A chemical that communicates information between members of the same species.

predator An animal that eats other animals for its nourishment.

Riker Mount A flat box used to store and display insects. It has a glass top for viewing and a cotton mat to cushion the insects.

scavenger An organism that consumes dead organic matter.

spiracles Openings through the insect's exoskeleton that lead to the tracheal system, to carry oxygen to the insect's cells.

stimulus An "event" that prompts a reaction or a response.

survey collection A collection of organisms from a certain habitat or area.

sweep net An insect collecting net designed to be swept through vegetation to collect large numbers of insects quickly.

tarsus The last (fifth) segment of the insect leg.

thorax The middle body division (of the three major body divisions) on which the legs and wings are attached.

tibia The fourth segment of the insect leg.

tracheal system A series of tubes throughout an insect's body that carry oxygen to the cells.

transfer aspirator A device that allows for the easy transfer of small insects from one area or container to another using suction.

trochanter The second segment of the insect leg.

wingpads The immature form of the insect wing, unable to produce flight.

Selected references

FIELD GUIDES

Borror, D.J. & R.E. White. *A Field Guide to the Insects of America North of Mexico.* Boston: Houghton Mifflin, 1970

Bland, R.G. & H.E. Jaques. *How to Know the Insects.* Dubuque, Iowa: W.C. Brown Co. Publ., 1978

Zim, H.S. & C. Cottam. *Insects, A Guide to Familiar American Insects.* NY: Simon & Schuster, 1951.

Arnett, R. & R. Jacques. *Simon & Schuster's Guide to Insects.* NY: Simon & Schuster, 1981.

Audubon Society & L. Milne. *The Audubon Society Field Guide to North American Insects & Spiders.* New York: Knopf, 1980

Borror, D.J. & D.M. DeLong. *A Field Guide to the Insects.* Peterson Field Guide. Boston: Houghton Mifflin, 1970

AQUATIC FIELD GUIDES

Lehmkuhl, D.M. *How to Know the Aquatic Insects.* Dubuque, Iowa: W.C. Brown Co. Publ., 1979

McCafferty, W.P. *Aquatic Entomology.* New York: Jones & Bartlett, 1982

Index

Other bestsellers of related interest

BOTANY: 49 Science Fair Projects
—*Robert L. Bonnet and G. Daniel Keen*
A rich source of project ideas for teachers, parents, and youth leaders, *Botany* introduces children ages 8 through 13 to the wonder and complexity of the natural world through worthwhile, and often environmentally timely, experimentation. Projects are grouped categorically under plant germination, photosynthesis, hydroponics, plant tropism, plant cells, seedless plants, and plant dispersal. Each experimentation contains a subject overview, materials list, problem identification, hypothesis, procedures and further research suggestions. Numerous illustrations and tables are included. 176 pages, 149 illustrations. Book No. 3277, $9.95 paperback, $16.95 hardcover

BOTANY: 49 MORE Science Fair Projects
—*Robert L. Bonnet and G. Daniel Keen*
This project idea book introduces children ages 8 through 13 to the wonder and complexity of the natural world through environmentally conscious experimentation. You'll find projects on temperature effects, hydrotropism, transpiration, seed germination, and more. 160 pages, illustrated. Book No. 3416, $9.95 paperback, $16.95 hardcover

EARTH SCIENCE: 49 Science Fair Projects
—*Robert L. Bonnet and G. Daniel Keen*
This is an excellent resource for cultivating a better understanding of planet Earth among children ages 8-13. By studying the forces at work around them, they develop an appreciation for the foundations of science—concise thinking, clear notes and data gathering, curiosity and patience—which can carry over to every aspect of their lives. Projects include: growing crystals, solar distillery; erosion, weather forecasting, and more. 160 pages, 43 illustrations. Book No. 3287, $9.95 paperback, $16.95 hardcover

ENVIRONMENTAL SCIENCE: 49 Science Fair Projects—*Robert L. Bonnet and G. Daniel Keen*
Here's a collection of fun educational projects that introduces children ages 8 through 13 to the effects of pollution, landfill decomposition, and water contamination, chemical waste, and environmentally stressed wildlife. All projects are designed for use in science fair competitions and include an outline, a hypothesis, a complete materials list, and step-by-step procedures. 140 pages, illustrated. Book No. 3369, $9.95 paperback, $16.95 hardcover

COMPUTERS: 49 Science Fair Projects
—*Robert L. Bonnet and G. Daniel Keen*
This collection of step-by-step science fair projects—using PCs and BASIC programming—challenges students ages 8 through 13 to think logically and apply the principles of scientific inquiry. Students will explore history, physics, math, and meteorology as they develop games of chance, aircraft design tests, mathematical conversions, and much more! 190 pages, 75 illustrations. Book No. 3524, $9.95 paperback, $16.95 hardcover

SPACE AND ASTRONOMY: 49 Science Fair Projects—*Robert L. Bonnet and G. Daniel Keen*
Spark your child's interest in space—and renew your own—with this treasure chest of discovery. It provides innovative home and classroom science projects designed specifically with science fair competitions in mind. The projects encompass a variety of subjects such as the observation of the heavens, clocks, calendars, time, the solar system, beyond the solar system, and meteorites. 144 pages, 32 illustrations. Book No. 3934, $9.95 paperback, $16.95 hardcover

SCIENCE FAIR: Developing a Successful and Fun Project—*Maxine Haren Iritz, Photographs by A. Frank Iritz*

Here's all the step-by-step guidance parents and teachers need to help students complete prize-quality science fair projects! This book provides easy-to-follow advice on every step of science fair project preparation from choosing a topic and defining the problem to conducting the experiment, drawing conclusions, and setting up the fair display. 96 pages, 83 illustrations. Book No. 2936, $9.95 paperback, $16.95 hardcover

200 ILLUSTRATED SCIENCE EXPERIMENTS FOR CHILDREN—*Robert J. Brown*

An ideal sourcebook for parents, teachers, club and scout leaders, or anyone who's fascinated with the wonders of science, this outstanding book is designed to make learning basic scientific principles exciting and fun. Literally crammed with different and interesting things to keep your youngsters entertained for hours, the collection of experiments presented here demonstrate such principles as sound, vibrations, mechanics, electricity, and magnetism. 196 pages, 200 illustrations. Book No. 2825, $9.95 paperback only

SCIENCE MAGIC FOR KIDS: 68 Simple & Safe Experiments—*William R. Wellnitz, Ph.D.*

An understanding and appreciation of science by youngsters in grades K-5 requires active, hands-on participation. Wellnitz provides dozens of simple simple projects that will help children discover the "magic" of science, learning basic scientific principles as they play with safe and inexpensive materials commonly found around the house. Projects include the chemistry of color, food and nutrition, properties of soap bubbles, and general biology. 128 pages, 102 illustrations. Book No. 3423, $9.95 paperback only

333 MORE SCIENCE TRICKS AND EXPERIMENTS—*Robert J. Brown*

Now, a second big collection of science "tricks" and demonstrations from the author of the popular syndicated newspaper column, *Science and You!* Designed to make learning basic scientific principles exciting and fun, this is an ideal sourcebook for parents, teachers, club and scout leaders . . . and just about anyone who's fascinated with the wonders of scientific and natural phenomena! 240 pages, 213 illustrations. Book No. 1835, $10.95 paperback only

333 SCIENCE TRICKS AND EXPERIMENTS —*Robert J. Brown*

"Well-described and aptly illustrated.
—*New Technical Books*

Here is a delightful collection of experiments and "tricks" that demonstrate a variety of well-known, and no so well-known, scientific principles and illusions. Find tricks based on inertia, momentum, and sound projects based on biology, water surface tension, gravity and centrifugal force, heat, and light. Every experiment is easy to understand and construct and uses ordinary household items. 208 pages, 189 illustrations. Book No. 1825, $9.95 paperback only

Look for These and Other TAB Books at Your Local Bookstore

To Order Call Toll Free 1-800-822-8158
(24-hour telephone service available.)

or write to TAB Books, Blue Ridge Summit, PA 17294-0840.

Title	Product No.	Quantity	Price

☐ Check or money order made payable to TAB Books

Charge my ☐ VISA ☐ MasterCard ☐ American Express

Acct. No. _____ Exp. _____

Signature: _____

Name: _____

Address: _____

City: _____

State: _____ Zip: _____

Subtotal $ _____

Postage and Handling
($3.00 in U.S., $5.00 outside U.S.) $ _____

Add applicable state and local
sales tax $ _____

TOTAL $ _____

TAB Books catalog free with purchase; otherwise send $1.00 in check or money order and receive $1.00 credit on your next purchase.

Orders outside U.S. must pay with international money in U.S. dollars drawn on a U.S. bank.

TAB Guarantee: If for any reason you are not satisfied with the book(s) you order, simply return it (them) within 15 days and receive a full refund.

BC